ACT-EAST
VIA THE NORTHEAST

How India's Northeast Is Strengthening The *Kizuna* (Bond) Between India, Japan and ASEAN ?

ACT-EAST
VIA THE NORTHEAST

How India's Northeast Is Strengthening The *Kizuna* (Bond) Between India, Japan and ASEAN ?

Dr. Rupakjyoti Borah

Foreword by
Prof. James Mayall
University of Cambridge

Delta Book World
New Delhi-110 002

ISBN: 978-93-85719-12-7
First Published in 2019

Published by **Abhishek Goel** on behalf of

Delta Book World
G-4, Prahlad House
4832/24, Ansari Road
New Delhi - 110 002 (India)

Tel.: 011-4707 2321, 2324 5799
E-mail: deltabookworld@gmail.com
Website: www.kaveribooks.com

PRINTED IN INDIA

Dedicated To

The Biggest Fighter,

My Wife, Maushumi

My Sister,

Rashmi (Majoni)

and My Friend

Rathindra

FOREWORD

Peripheral areas of important states tend to exercise a disproportionate influence on the fate of the national population. Commanding the land and/or maritime borders with neighbours has traditionally given them certain advantages; their people often have cultural, linguistic and family ties across the border and can act as a bridgehead not only for the import and export of goods and services but also of ideas, both sacred and profane, and the tastes and fashions of material culture on which so much international cooperation depends. Controlling the high passes in traditional societies may have brought these advantages but it also carried risks of invasion or hostile infiltration from predatory neighbours, considerations which have often led to the militarisation of borders and created opportunities for local resistance and conflict. In some of these respects, although not the last, the North Eastern states of India have long been something of an enigmatic anomaly – a minority region, at a distance both geographically and culturally from the centres of mainstream Indian political culture, the region has suffered from economic and political neglect, and its intrinsic political and geo-economic significance has been largely neglected.

Now at last the political landscape is changing. The rise of China over the past quarter of a century, followed more recently by India's rapid development has concentrated Indian minds – but also those in the wider region and in international society more generally – on both the opportunities and risks involved in India's necessary coexistence with its northern neighbour. It simply makes no sense to continue ignoring the North East which is the natural bridge to South East Asia on the one hand and to consolidating the economic and political aspects of India's increasingly important strategic relationship with Japan. But old habits of mind as well as behaviour die hard so that one cannot rely on rhetoric alone to change realities on the ground. North East India needs a major investment not just of economic resources – crucial as that undoubtedly is – but also of political empathy and commitment.

Dr Rupakjyoti Borah, who comes from the region and knows it intimately as only someone with deep roots in a human as well as topographical environment can, has already established an international reputation as a serious strategic thinker on India's relationships in its Asian neighbourhood. He is the ideal guide to the complexities, challenges and opportunities posed by the Indian North East.

Central governments are as a rule resistant to

interference from their regions in the monopoly they hold over foreign and defence policy; and understandably so. They cannot always avoid it however, and in some cases there is a natural congruence between the interests of the State and those of the region. The Indian North East is one of these. Let us not be naïve: there is a huge amount of work to be done by those in the North East, as well as in the Government of India itself, if building the natural bridge between India and its eastern neighbourhood, is to be effectively accomplished. It is easy, sitting a long way off, and with no personal stake in the region, to lay down the law. That is not my intention. But I have no hesitation in saying that this short book, packed full of useful information on India's strategic Indian Ocean policy, the dilemmas of its relations with China, and the need to take positive steps to maximise the economic and diplomatic opportunities that the North East offers to Indian foreign policy, deserves not only to be widely read, but to make a major contribution to the policy debate on the next steps in India's "Act East" policy.

Prof. James Mayall
Sidney Sussex College,
Cambridge, U.K.

ACKNOWLEDGEMENTS

I have many people to thank who helped me through the process of writing this book. At the outset, I would like to thank the Chairman, Institute of South Asian Studies (ISAS), National University of Singapore, Ambassador Gopinath Pillai, Director, Prof. C Raja Mohan, Senior Associate Director, Mr Hernaikh Singh, Ambassador Iftikhar Chowdhury, Dr Duvvuri Subbarao, Dr Rani Mullen and all my other colleagues at the Institute of South Asian Studies (ISAS), National University of Singapore (NUS). Then, I would like to thank Yasuo Naito-san in Japan who allowed me to use some of the material, which I had earlier published in the *Japan Forward* website. I also have to thank many other people in Japan. These include my mentors, Vice Admiral (retd.) Hideaki Kaneda, Prof. Michimi Muranushi, Go Yamada-san, Prof. Maseteru Hino, Prof. Chiharu Takenaka, Eitaro Kojima, Prof. Atsushi Kato, Mrs Akiko MacDonald, Akihiko Takagi-sensei among others. I would also like to thank my good friend Takabumi Suzuoki-san for his valuable time and observations. I would also like to thank the Japan Institute of International Affairs (JIIA), which was my first point of contact in Japan, way back in 2011.

In the United Kingdom, I would like to thank Prof. James Mayall from the University of Cambridge who agreed to write the foreword of this book, in spite of his extremely hectic schedule. In India, I would like to thank Mr Ananth Krishna, my teacher Jugal Borah Sir, my friends Rathindra Sarma, Namsidimbo Zeliang, Prof. Man Mohini Kaul, Naoki Kumagai-san, Hideki Asari-san, H.E. Ambassador Chutintorn Sam Gongsakdi, Ambassador of Thailand to India, among others. In addition, I would also to thank Hiroshi Honjo-san, Satoru Nagao-san and Ambassador Aftab Seth, former Indian Ambassador to Japan. In Vietnam, I would like to thank Dr Le Thi Hang Nga and Prof. Nguyen Xuan Trung.

I would also like to thank my aunty Ms Purnima Borah and my uncle Hemendra Kumar Borah. Last, but not the least, my thanks go to my mother, Mrs Chitra Borah, father Dr Hiranya Kumar Borah, my two boys, elder son, Hurjyudoy Borah and younger son, Bishwabhiraj Borah and my very patient and ever-smiling wife, Maushumi. I would also like to thank my in-laws, Gautam Borgohain, Anubha Borgohain. My wife is an Ahom, whose ancestors are originally said to have migrated from Southeast Asia and this has lent a personal connection to my research. It is worth mentioning here that the Ahoms were the longest ruling dynasty in India.

Lastly, I, alone am responsible for all the mistakes in this.

Dr Rupakjyoti Borah

CONTENTS

PREFACE

On a flight between my hometown, Guwahati, in Northeast India and my workplace, Singapore, I was flabbergasted to note that the flight would be heading east to Imphal (in Manipur, Northeast India), before then heading west to New Delhi. We then headed eastward again to the final destination (my place of work), Singapore. What a waste of time and energy, I thought!

This got me thinking-why Northeast India, which is so close to the ASEAN region, is geographically so far removed from it? This part of the country has close filial ties with the ASEAN countries, especially with tribes like the Nagas spread across both sides of the border (in India and Myanmar). Northeast Indian states (Arunachal Pradesh, Nagaland, Manipur and Mizoram) share an approximately 1600 km border with Myanmar– which by the way, had also been a British colony.

Some of the Mizo tribes are also spread across the border in Myanmar. In the historical past, some Assamese princesses were married off to the royal family in Myanmar. Besides, as we head to the eastern and northern reaches of Arunachal Pradesh, the Buddhist influence becomes ever more apparent. In upper Assam, there is a village known as the Tai-phake village where the villagers have kept their customs and culture intact, just like their counterparts in some parts of Southeast Asia.

This led me to analyse threadbare why the Northeast is so disconnected from the ASEAN in spite of its physical proximity? What will it take for the Northeast Indian states to join the rest of India in the march for development and act as a bridge between India and the ASEAN and also between India and Japan? On the other hand, the Japanese have already had a historical presence in the Northeast and this has only increased in the present times. In doing so, it will not be doing anything new, but will be going back to the times when this part of the country acted as a bridge between South and Southeast Asia and also between South and East Asia.

WHAT'S IN IT FOR THE PEOPLE OF NORTHEAST INDIA ?

For the people of the Northeastern states, the last few years have been one of big changes. While the earlier generations of Northeasterners (including myself), had to make their way to the bigger Indian cities (like Delhi, Mumbai, Kolkata, Bangalore, or Pune) by train which often took 1/2/3 nights depending on the distance (and if there were *bandhs/hartals* etc), things have completely changed ever since air travel became more affordable.

Northeast Indians have a high level of English-speaking skills and this has seen them getting jobs in the hospitality industry in different parts of the country. Many youngsters from this region have moved to the bigger Indian cities and this has been made possible by the availability of cheaper air travel.

This has also resulted in some changes on the societal front too. Many youngsters from different parts of the Northeast have intermarried with people from other parts of India. Then, there is another sector which has seen a rapid induction of people from the Northeast-this is the private security services. I have been surprised to see security guards from the Northeastern states in the southern states of India–which is understandable, in the light of the fact that people from states like Kerala have moved to other countries in the Gulf region in search of more well-paying jobs.

The rapid improvement of road and air links between Northeast India and the ASEAN countries should lead to a sharp increase in the number of people from the ASEAN countries visiting the Northeastern states. With rising income levels, many residents from the Northeastern states are already visiting the ASEAN countries. In addition, youths from these parts of the country could also find jobs in the ASEAN countries, especially in the hospitality sector. Then there is the medical tourism sector, where patients from the ASEAN countries are availing healthcare services in Northeast India.

Northeastern states produce very good quality of handicrafts which can find a market in the ASEAN countries especially because of the similarity of designs, prints etc. In addition, produce from the Northeast like tea, timber, coal, sand etc can have a ready market available in the ASEAN countries. This is likely to improve further as direct connectivity has now been established between India and Myanmar through the opening of land-routes.

After all, as the crow flies, Guwahati in Northeast India would be much closer to Mandalay in Myanmar, than say to Mumbai in western India.

This book is divided into the following chapters:

Chapter 1: Introduction

This will introduce the contents of my book. It will look at why Northeast India is crucial in India's growing connectivity with both ASEAN as well as Japan and explain the rationale behind this book, especially in the light of India's "Act-East Policy".

Chapter 2: India's Links with ASEAN

This chapter will explore the huge opportunities that have emerged ever since the launch of the "Act-East Policy" (earlier known as the "Look-East Policy") in the early 1990's in the wake of India's balance of payments crisis and the dissolution of the erstwhile Soviet Union. India has moved a long way ever since it became a sectoral dialogue partner of the ASEAN in 1992. Earlier, in 2017, India and ASEAN celebrated 25 years of their dialogue partnership.

Chapter 3: India-Japan Ties

This chapter will look at India's growing ties with Japan and Tokyo's infrastructure projects in Northeast

India. Northeast India is a region where India's "Act-East Policy" meets Japan's "Free and Open Indo-Pacific strategy." In the light of both India and Japan not joining the China-backed Belt and Road Initiative (BRI), cooperation in the realm of infrastructure between India and Japan is only going to increase in the near future.

Chapter 4: Importance of the Maritime Domain in Japan-India-ASEAN Ties

This chapter will look at the importance of the maritime domain in the ties between NE India, ASEAN and Japan. At the Delhi Dialogue X-held in July 2018 in New Delhi, the theme was "Strengthening ASEAN-India Maritime Cooperation". Maritime links will acquire critical importance in the years ahead as New Delhi increasingly looks at the maritime domain, as it is left with relatively lesser options on land. The maritime domain will assume increasing importance once projects like the Indian-funded Kaladan Multi-Modal Transportation Corridor project in Myanmar reach fruition. This is because it will provide an access to the sea to the landlocked Northeastern states of the country via the Kaladan river in Bangladesh. This will also be an alternative to the narrow chicken's neck corridor which joins the Northeastern states to the mainland near Siliguri in West Bengal.

Chapter 5: The US and China Factors

This chapter will look at the China factor as India's Northeast expands its connections with both ASEAN as well as Japan. Beijing claims the Indian state of Arunachal Pradesh and has not been too happy, especially in the light of the growing Japanese involvement in Northeast India. Beijing has important interests in India's neighbourhood especially in Myanmar and also in Bangladesh, though things have changed slightly ever since a civilian government took office in Myanmar. Arunachal Pradesh shares borders with China and in 1962, Chinese troops invaded India through Arunachal Pradesh. Since then, Sino-Indian relations have undergone a change and the trust-deficit has been difficult to fill. The chapter will also analyse the growing ties between India and the US and its impact on India-Japan-ASEAN ties.

Chapter 6: A 20-Point Agenda For 2020

The final chapter will look at the road ahead as India's Northeast emerges as a strategic gateway not only between India and ASEAN, but also between India and Japan. It will also include a set of recommendations which will help in bringing Northeast India, ASEAN and Japan ever more closer.

Importance of this Book

India's relations with both Japan and ASEAN have been growing rapidly as a result of the "Act-East Policy". While inaugurating India's third Indian Agriculture Research Institute (IARI) at Gogamukh in Upper Assam in May 2017, PM Modi noted that "Northeast was known as NE, but from now on it will be known as new economy, new energy, new empowerment – in a way it will become a new engine for India's growth."[1]

The North Eastern states are also beginning to court foreign investment as seen in the maiden Global Investors' Summit in Guwahati, Assam earlier in February 2018. The government of Assam has also inked an agreement with the National Building Construction Corporation (NBCC) to set up a 65-storey Twin Towers, in Guwahati, Assam which is being touted as the hub of India's engagement efforts with the ASEAN countries as a part of its "Act-East Policy".

At the inauguration of India's longest bridge over the Lohit river in Assam (on the third anniversary of his swearing in as the Prime Minister on May 26, 2017), PM Modi noted that "the eastern and north-eastern parts of the country have the greatest potential for economic development, and this bridge is just one element of the Union Government's vision in this regard."[2]

The development of Northeast India will also be in keeping with the present government's strategy of "Neighbourhood First" as Bhutan and Nepal were the first two countries, which PM Modi visited after taking over as the PM. In addition, PM Modi had invited the Heads of State of all the SAARC countries to his inauguration.

However, although the total trade between India and ASEAN stood at around US$ 81.33 billion (approximately 10.6 per cent of India's total external trade), Northeast India only accounts for a miniscule portion of it, in spite of this geographical contiguity. On the other hand, in another worrying development-India made up only 2.6 per cent of ASEAN's total external trade in 2016.[3] In order to bring up development levels in Northeast India to levels in other parts of the country, cooperation with ASEAN and Japan is *sine-qua-non.* Only this will ensure that this region will able to overcome what many observers call "the tyranny of geography".

NOTES

1. *The Hindustan Times,* Northeast should be the 'New Engine' for India's growth: Narendra Modi in Assam, available at https://www.hindustantimes.com/india-news/northeast-should-be-the-new-engine-for-india-s-growth-narendra-modi-in-assam/story-iT7zgfARNbT0zGhRLvGYoL.html accessed on10 February 2019.
2. PM Narendra Modi speech, available at https://www.narendramodi.in/pm-modi-to-inaugurate-dhola-sadia-bridge-across-river-brahamputra-in-purana-sadiya-assam-535589 accessed on 10 February 2019.
3. The Straits Times, "Asean and India: 25 years and beyond", https://www.businesstimes.com.sg/opinion/asean-and-india-25-years-and-beyond accessed on 20 January 2019.

1

INTRODUCTION

The Northeastern region of India–which includes the states of Sikkim, Arunachal Pradesh, Nagaland, Manipur, Mizoram, Tripura, Assam and Meghalaya – are sometimes known as the seven sisters (before Sikkim came to be included as part of the NE). These states cover an area of 2,63,179 sq. km, which constitutes approximately eight percent of the country's total geographical area. The region houses around 3.76 per cent of the total population of India.[1]

These states receive the first sunrise in India. It is worth pointing out here that the literal translation of the name of the Northeastern state of Arunachal Pradesh is "the land of the dawn-lit mountains". This name could not have been more apt as Dong in Arunachal Pradesh gets the first sunrise in India.[2]

The states of Northeast India share international borders with Nepal, Bhutan, China, Myanmar and Bangladesh and are joined to the rest of the country by the narrow Siliguri Corridor – also known as the Chicken's Neck – a stretch of around 200 kms which varies in breadth from 27 to 60 km.

Home to many tribes and people of varied ethnicities and religions, this region has now been pitch forked into national and international headlines with the launch of India's "Act-East Policy"– earlier known as the "Look-East Policy". There are many sectors in Northeast India, which have tremendous potential. These include the hydroelectricity sector, tourism, horticulture, floriculture, the hospitality sector etc.

In terms of geography, Northeast India ranges from the sweaty plains and the swamps of Assam to the snow-capped Himalayan peaks in Arunachal Pradesh. Geopolitically, its importance cannot be underestimated. Northeast India is an essential element of the "Act-East Policy" which aims to be a bridge between India and ASEAN and also between India and Japan. The "Act-East Policy" has had bipartisan support from different political parties in India and has enjoyed a significant measure of success. New Delhi's ties with ASEAN have also travelled a long way in the period since it became a sectoral dialogue partner of the ASEAN back in 1992. It went on to become a full dialogue partner of the ASEAN in 1995. It became a member of the East Asia Summit in 2005, in which countries like Singapore and Japan played a very helpful role.

However, this region has not escaped the pulls and pressures of international geopolitics. China has claims over the Northeast Indian state of Arunachal Pradesh and has raised objections whenever the Dalai Lama has visited the border state. This region's importance can be easily seen in the way New Delhi reacted when Chinese troops started constructing a road in the Doklam region of Bhutan (claimed by China), thereby threatening the narrow chicken's neck corridor. The subsequent standoff between the two sides rocked the region and the rest of the world, until thankfully the two countries began to pull back their forces just before the BRICS Summit in Xiamen, which was attended by the Indian PM Narendra Modi.

While New Delhi earlier had an almost conscious policy of keeping the infrastructure in India's Northeastern region underdeveloped (due to threats from China), there has been a significant change in the lookout on the part of Indian government, especially after the Modi government took office in India. Since 1962, when Chinese forces attacked Indian forces in the region (before withdrawing unconditionally), the region has been suffering from lack of connectivity. Many parts of the Northeast remain cut-off, especially in the summer months when the monsoon strikes this region.

However, many new construction projects are now being undertaken in the region.

1. The Bhupen Hazarika Setu

In May 2017, PM Narendra Modi inaugurated India's longest road bridge (9.15 kms) across the Lohit river in Assam. This has fulfilled a long-standing demand of the people of this region and will be a big help in connecting, not only some far-flung parts of Assam, but also in connecting the remote but extremely important state of Arunachal Pradesh.

2. The Trans-Arunachal Highway

This highway will extend all the way from Tawang in the western part of Arunachal Pradesh to Kanubari in the east and will finally meet with the National Highway-52 near Bogibeel in upper Assam, providing seamless connectivity between the different parts of this frontier state. This will also make it easier for the residents of the eastern parts of Arunachal Pradesh to connect to Dibrugarh in Assam on the southern bank of the Brahmaputra. Dibrugarh is an important railway hub and also houses an airport which connects to different parts of the country.

3. The Bogibeel Bridge

The Bogibeel bridge connects Dibrugarh on the southern bank of the Brahmaputra in Assam to Dhemaji on the northern bank of the state. This 4.94 km bridge is the longest rail-cum-road bridge in India. The Bogibeel bridge is a part of the Central government's ambitious initiative to improve connectivity in both Assam and the neighbouring state of Arunachal Pradesh. While earlier, people have been making this crossing by boat, it was not safe to do so during the monsoon months because of the increase in water levels. In addition, earlier vehicles had to take a almost 500 km detour via the Koliabhomora bridge near Tezpur to go to the North Bank. This bridge was inaugurated on 25th December last year, on the birth anniversary of the former Indian PM, Atal Behari Vajpayee.

4. India's Longest Bridge – approx. 20 kms Across

This bridge will be India's longest bridge when

completed (between Dhubri in Assam and Phulbari in Meghalaya) and is going to be financed by the Japan International Cooperation Agency (JICA) – this is also a symbol of the growing cooperation between India and Japan.

5. The India-Myanmar-Thailand (IMT) Trilateral Highway

The India-Myanmar-Thailand (IMT) trilateral highway is planned to connect Moreh in Manipur to Mae Sot in Thailand. There are also proposals to extend it all the way to Vietnam through pre-existing highways. The IMT trilateral highway is set to connect with the East-West Economic corridor which runs from the Myanmarese port city of Mawlamyine all the way to Da Nang in Vietnam. The East West Economic Corridor extends includes five countries – Myanmar, Thailand, Laos, Cambodia and Vietnam.

WHY NORTHEAST INDIA IS KEY FOR INDIA-ASEAN TIES ?

Northeast India is acquiring a new salience in the light of Delhi's non-participation in the Beijing-led One Belt One Road (OBOR) initiative (also known as the Belt and Road initiative). As it is not enough for New Delhi to only refuse to join the BRI, it must provide an alternative model as well. Hence, closer connectivity with Southeast Asia will be very important for India.

India has lent a $1 billion line of credit to the ASEAN as a whole for digital and physical connectivity programmes. Addressing the plenary session of the India–Association of Southeast Asian Nations (ASEAN)

Commemorative Summit earlier in January last year, India's Prime Minister, Narendra Modi, noted the importance of our (ASEAN-India) Strategic Partnership, "placing ASEAN at the centre of India's Act-East Policy".[3]

Indeed, from the days of yore, India has had close ties with the ASEAN member-states. However, the two sides grew apart in the period after India's independence in 1947, as many of the Southeast Asian nations inched closer to the Western bloc whereas New Delhi adopted a non-aligned foreign policy and, later on, grew close to the former Soviet Union, especially with the signing of the Treaty of Peace, Friendship and Cooperation with the erstwhile Union of Soviet Socialist Republic (USSR) in 1971. However, all this changed after the dissolution of the former Soviet Union and the end of the Cold War in the early 1990's.

These events forced New Delhi to completely overhaul its foreign policy. The 'Look-East Policy', as it was then called, was launched by the government of the former Indian Prime Minister Narasimha Rao – to reach out to countries of Southeast and East Asia besides the wider Asia-Pacific region. It was subsequently continued by PM Narasimha Rao's successors, including the National Democratic Alliance (NDA) governments. It was renamed as the "Act-East Policy" after the Modi government took office in India in May 2014.

In the present times, with the term 'Indo-Pacific' gaining increasing currency worldwide in both scholarly and official circles, ASEAN-India ties have assumed greater salience. At the same time, countries across the world (especially in Asia) are adjusting to the rise of China. The ASEAN member-states are no different. Many of them have huge trading volumes with China, but at the same time, are embroiled in territorial disputes with Beijing. It is little surprise that they are looking at diversifying their foreign policy options and the rise of India has given this opportunity.

WHY TIES WITH JAPAN ARE GROWING ?

At the same time, India's relations with Japan have also been growing steadily, especially after Prime Minister Shinzo Abe came to power in Japan in December 2012 for a second term in office. Japan is investing in a big way in the development of infrastructure in Northeast India and this is where Japan's "Free and Open Indo-Pacific Strategy" meets India's "Act-East Policy".

Japan has a historical connect with the north-eastern part of India, dating back to the Second World War when soldiers from Netaji Subhash Chandra Bose's Indian National Army (INA) hoisted the Indian tricolour for the first time on Indian soil in the North-eastern state of Manipur before they were beaten back by Allied Forces in the Battles of Imphal and Kohima. However, in the present times, this cooperation has taken on a different character, especially in the light of Japan and India's non-participation in the Beijing-led One Belt One Road (OBOR) initiative.

Tokyo has its own "Partnership for Quality

Infrastructure" initiative while New Delhi is developing ports like the Chabahar Port in Iran. Meanwhile, India and Japan are now collaborating in the field of infrastructure, in India and are planning to collaborate in other countries like Sri Lanka.

One of the important facets of New Delhi's growing ties with Tokyo has been the burgeoning cooperation between Japan and India's Northeast. As noted earlier, the contract for the almost 20-km Dhubri-Phulbari bridge in Northeast India has been awarded. When completed, it will become India's longest bridge, surpassing the Bhupen Hazarika Setu in Assam, which is 9.15 kms across. Funded by the Japan International Cooperation Agency (JICA), the proposed Dhubri-Phulbari bridge is emblematic of the growing involvement of Japan in India's Northeast.

Northeast India has lagged behind many other parts of the country in terms of development. However, India's "Act-East Policy" (known earlier as the "Look-East Policy") has come as a harbinger of hope for the Northeast, especially as New Delhi has increased its engagement with countries in the ASEAN region and also with countries like Japan. As part of its increased engagement with the ASEAN nations, New Delhi is also investing in improving infrastructure in Myanmar and is involved in the India-Myanmar-Thailand (IMT) trilateral highway. Tokyo has already been closely involved economically in ASEAN countries like Myanmar, a country which also serves as India's land-bridge to the ASEAN region.

CONFLUENCE OF INTERESTS OF INDIA, JAPAN AND ASEAN IN NORTHEAST INDIA

During the visit of Japanese Prime Minister Shinzo Abe to India in September 2017, the two countries "welcomed the India-Japan cooperation on development of India's North Eastern Region (NER) as a concrete symbol of developing synergies between India's "Act East Policy" and Japan's "Free and Open Indo Pacific Strategy."

Under PM Abe, Japan has embarked on the "Free and Open Indo-Pacific Strategy" which aims at "promoting connectivity between Asia, the Middle East and Africa." It actually builds on PM Abe's landmark speech before the Indian Parliament in August 2007 (during his earlier term in office) titled "Confluence of the Two Seas" where he noted that "the Pacific and the Indian Oceans are now bringing about a dynamic coupling as seas of freedom and of prosperity."

With regards to Northeast India, Japan has contributed Official Development Assistance (ODA) loans for the North East Road Network Connectivity Improvement Project and will extend a loan to the tune of approximately Rs 2239 crore. It is also involved in initiatives like the Guwahati water supply scheme and the Nagaland Forest Management Project.

The Japanese government also has a programme known as the IRIS programme, which has seen young talents from the Northeastern part of India, visit Japan. The IRIS programme is named after "a mysterious link between Japan and the North East Region of India, i.e., one species of iris called Kombirei that grows mainly around Loktak Lake near Imphal and commonly used in festivals and was found to be a new species in India and identical with Kakitsubata which was known as "Japanese IRIS".[4]

In addition, Japan has also been trying to improve its ties with the Himalayan Kingdom of Bhutan of late. The Japanese Foreign Minister Taro Kono made the first-ever visit by a Japanese Minster to Bhutan in June last year. A Japanese agricultural expert Mr. Nishioka was dispatched to Bhutan way back in 1964 (long before diplomatic relations had been established) and he lived in Bhutan for 28 years before passing away. He was fondly regarded as "Dasho Nishioka" in Bhutan. The current King of Bhutan had visited Fukushima after the Great East Japan Earthquake of March 2011.

NOT A SMOOTH ROAD AHEAD

However, there may be quite a few challenges for both Tokyo and New Delhi as they join forces to give a leg-up to infrastructure development in India's Northeastern region.

First, the states (provinces) in Northeast India suffer from lack of good quality infrastructure. These states require a huge and sustained infusion of capital in the infrastructure sector.

Second, employment opportunities are few and far between, while levels of literacy in the Northeast are relatively higher than many other parts of the country. This has created a problem of unemployment among educated youths. Though insurgency has waned considerably, there are still some cases of extortion in some of the Northeastern states.

Third, the Northeastern states regularly suffer from floods, landslides, mudslides etc., which bring immense misery to the people of the region and severely impact the already-existing infrastructure in the region. It will, therefore, also be a challenge to maintain the newly-built infrastructure in the region.

Fourth, the projects will require adequate coordination between the different state governments of Northeast India, an area where there have been issues in the past.

The slew of infrastructure projects being undertaken by Japan and India in the Northeastern region of India is a clear indicator of the growing bonhomie between the two countries. Japan and India will also cooperate in India's strategic Andaman and Nicobar islands. The fact that Japan has been allowed to invest in the strategically important Northeastern region of India and the Andaman and Nicobar islands points to the growing trust-levels between the two countries. Tokyo has also been involved in many other flagship infrastructure development projects in India like the Mumbai-Ahemdabad Bullet Train Project, the Delhi-Mumbai Industrial Corridor, the Chennai-Bangalore Industrial Corridor, the Delhi Metro and many others.

HAVE THINGS CHANGED NOW ?

Both ASEAN and Japan are looking at India and especially India's Northeast in a new light. This is to do with both economic and strategic reasons. Some of the ASEAN nations have been embroiled in the South China Sea dispute with China. On the other hand, countries like Vietnam and the Philippines have been bearing the brunt of this rising assertiveness on the part of Beijing. India has always been present in the region and hence for New Delhi, it is a homecoming of sorts. Even in the heart of Muslim-majority Indonesia, one finds pockets of Indian influence like the Bali island. In fact, the influence of Hinduism and Buddhism seeped through right through the ASEAN region. In the case of the different versions of the Ramayana which are performed in Thailand and Indonesia, it is a delight to see how it has been enriched by the infusion of local customs and culture.

Part of the reason is also economic, given the rapid growth of the Indian economy and the immense opportunities that it provides. Northeast India's physical proximity to the ASEAN countries has raised the interest of both policy makers and ordinary citizens in these countries.

When it comes to Japan, it has been trying to claw its way back into the international sweepstakes after PM Shinzo Abe came back to power for a second term. Tokyo has a territorial dispute with Beijing over the Japanese-controlled Senkaku islands (claimed as Diaoyu by China). In addition, Tokyo has not joined the Beijing-backed Asian Infrastructure Investment Bank (AIIB) and has also not joined the Belt and Road initiative, though it has expressed its willingness to cooperate with China on a case-by-case basis.

NEW DELHI'S FOREIGN POLICY PRIORITIES

What now begs the question is that, going forward, what are major foreign policy priorities for India in 2019 ?

The first challenge for New Delhi would undoubtedly be to manage its relations with China. The Doklam standoff earlier in 2017 showed that friction between the two Asian behemoths could take place again, as both them are growing economically and militarily at the same time.

Second, India's relations with Pakistan and the neighbouring SAARC nations will also demand attention from New Delhi. While PM Modi started off with a flourish when he invited the heads of state of all the neighbouring SAARC nations to his inauguration, since then much water has flowed down the Ganges. Sri Lanka has also been increasingly getting cosier with Beijing, in spite of New Delhi focussing greater attention and resources on the Island nation. In addition, India also faces issues arising from the influx of Rohingya refugees, which is related to civil strife in Myanmar.

Third, increasing its economic engagement with the ASEAN nations and also with Africa will be key to maintaining New Delhi's economic growth at present levels. This will help New Delhi decrease its huge trade deficit with China. At the same time, India will have to get more manufacturing done in India, in order to create jobs for its young populace, in case it is to take advantage of its demographic dividend.

Fourth, relations with Japan have been on an all-high time but the challenge for both the countries will now be to implement all the deals that have been signed. The Mumbai-Ahmedabad Shinkansen project and the many infrastructure projects being undertaken with Japanese assistance in India will demand attention from both the governments. During the visit of PM Modi to Japan last year, India and Japan signed a currency-swap agreement for $75 billon dollars. However, trade levels between the two countries is abysmally low and this demands proactive steps from both the governments and private corporations.

Fifth, ensuring a steady supply of energy will be key for India. New Delhi is importing energy from a host of countries across the world like the Central Asian nations, Australia, Indonesia, Africa besides the Gulf countries and now also from the US. Supplies can be volatile at times, especially from the Gulf countries and hence New Delhi needs to find out alternate sources of energy, besides going in for less-polluting ones. This is where the civilian nuclear deal with Japan and other similar deals will be very critical.

Sixth, on the security front, it will be important for India not just to face traditional security threats, but also to prepare for non-traditional security threats. Climate change would pose a key question to Indian policy makers. New Delhi also needs to protect the interests of the huge Indian Diaspora spread across different parts of the world and this will be a key test of Indian diplomacy as sometimes Indian national interests could well be at odds with the interests of the host nation. Indians have also been caught up in conflict zones like Iraq, Syria and Yemen and the government has done a commendable job, in being able to rescue Indians stranded in such conflict zones.

Seventh, as a rising global power, India will be called in to take a stand on key international issues, more often than in the past and unlike earlier, New Delhi may no longer be able to afford to be a fence sitter on key international issues. In the light of its growing ties with Israel, ties with the Arab countries will require a delicate balancing act.

With more and more nations, including the US, using the terminology "Indo-Pacific" last year, it seems that India's importance in the foreign policy calculus of most nations will increase.

Ever since the end of the Cold War, Japan-India relations have seen tremendous progress. Stronger Japan-India relations have cross party support in India and this is the biggest advantage for the bilateral ties. Indian Justice Radha Binod Pal had spoken in favour of the Japanese during the Tokyo Trials held in the aftermath of the Second World War and is still revered in Japan for the same. Another notable factor is that in the case of Japan-India relations, the past does not crop up in the present as their relationship is not clouded by historical issues.

Although there was a thaw in the relations in the wake of India's nuclear tests in 1998, the ties made a turn around during the visit of the then Japanese Prime Minister Yoshiro Mori to India in the year 2000. Thereafter, in

2006, the bilateral relationship was upgraded to a "Strategic and Global Partnership"[5].

It was during Shinzo Abe's earlier stint as the Prime Minister in 2007 when he outlined his vision for Japan-India ties in his famous speech "Confluence of the Two Seas"[6] in the Indian Parliament. In this speech, he mentioned that "by Japan and India coming together in this way, this "broader Asia" will evolve into an immense network spanning the entirety of the Pacific Ocean, incorporating the United States of America and Australia. Open and transparent, this network will allow people, goods, capital, and knowledge to flow freely."[7]

JAPAN'S FOREIGN POLICY PRIORITIES

Japan under PM Abe has been caught between a rock and a hard place. While on the one hand, the US (in spite of being a treaty ally) has imposed some tariffs on Japan, on the political front, rapid developments in the Korean peninsula, have put it in a difficult diplomatic situation. On the other hand, China has been becoming more aggressive in the areas around Japan while in spite of the best efforts of PM Abe, the relations with Russia are no better.

No wonder Japan has been looking to the ASEAN and to countries like India. The ASEAN region is important for Japan because Japanese companies have a close economic partnership with the ASEAN countries, especially in countries like Vietnam, Thailand and Singapore. Besides, Myanmar has emerged as an enticing market for Japanese companies because it is a largely unexplored market. Myanmar has been trying very hard to balance the Asian giants like India, China and Japan. While it has historical ties with India given the Buddhist angle and the fact that both India and Myanmar were British colonies, China is a giant neighbour that Myanmar cannot afford to ignore.

DEVELOPMENT PROCESS IN NORTHEAST INDIA

North-east India has overcome a tumultuous period in its history. In the early 1980's, Assam, which is the largest state in NE India (in terms of its population), was engulfed by strife in the wake of the anti-foreigner agitation in the state which partially ended with the signing of the Assam Accord in 1985. It was in Nagaland that insurgency reared its ugly head, way back around the time of India's independence. Things did not end in Assam with the signing of the Assam Accord. Thereafter too, a long period of violence followed which finally ended in many ways when the Indian Army conducted a massive operation in the jungles of Bhutan along with their Bhutanese counterparts.

In Nagaland too, the major Naga insurgent outfits are in ceasefire with the Central Government. This situation was also repeated in states like Manipur. Mizoram in Northeast India has had its own bout of insurgency, which ended with the signing of the Mizo Accord.

Another important issue in the region in illegal immigration from Bangladesh. New Delhi is not in a position to tackle this issue on its own and hence would need the support of neighbouring countries like Bangladesh in this regard and hence cooperation with the neighbouring countries in crucial for India.

In the future with adequate investment by the Centre, the Northeast could very well be a power-surplus part of India and could in fact sell the excess power to other countries, especially neighbouring countries like Myanmar and Bangladesh. This would help fill up the coffers of the North-eastern states, many of whom rely on support from the Central government in order to undertake various developmental activities.

One of the main factors, which led to the rise of insurgency in Northeast India, is the lack of employment opportunities for the youths of the region and this is where cooperation with ASEAN will be key for the North-eastern governments.

NOTES

1. http://www.ncert.nic.in/publication/Miscellaneous/pdf_files/tinei101.pdf accessed on 12 February 2019.
2. The Times of India, "This is where the sun rises first in India", https://timesofindia.indiatimes.com/india/This-is-where-the-sun-rises-first-in-India/articleshow/53381054.cms accessed on 15 February 2019.
3. The Economic Times, "India, ASEAN leaders agree to boost maritime cooperation" available ateconomictimes.indiatimes.com/articleshow/62654982.cms?utm_source=contentofinterest&utm_mediutext & utm_campaign=cppst accessed on 20 January 2019.

4. Embassy of Japan in India, "IRIS Program: Ambassador Hiramatsu saw off 23 young talents from Manipur and Nagaland visiting Japan", available at https://www.in.emb-japan.go.jp/itpr_en/00_000442.html accessed on 21 February 2019.
5. Ministry of External Affairs, "India, Prime Minister Shinzo Abe's visit: pinnacle of India-Japan Relations" available at http://www.mea.gov.in/in-focus-article.htm? 22762/Prime+Minister+Shinzo+Abes+visit+pinnacle+of+IndiaJapan+ relations accessed on 12 January 2019.
6. Ministry of Foreign Affairs, Japan, "Confluence of the Two Seas", Speech by H.E. Mr. Shinzo Abe, Prime Minister of Japan at the Parliament of the Republic of India, available at http://www.mofa.go.jp/region/asia-paci/pmv0708/speech-2.html accessed on 11 January 2019.
7. ibid.

2

INDIA'S LINKS WITH ASEAN

Northeast India has lagged behind many other parts of the country in terms of development. However, India's "Act-East Policy" (known earlier as the "Look-East Policy") offers new hope to the Northeast, as New Delhi increases its engagement with countries in the ASEAN region and with Japan.

India's ties with ASEAN have developed at a fast pace ever since New Delhi became a sectoral dialogue partner of the ASEAN in 1992, a Dialogue Partner in 1996 and then going on to become a summit-level partner in 2002. The relationship was upgraded to a Strategic Partnership in 2012.

WHAT IS THE "ACT-EAST POLICY" ABOUT?

When India launched the "Look-East Policy" in the early 1990's in the light of the balance of payments crisis and the dissolution of the erstwhile Soviet Union, one part of the country that stood to benefit the most from it was Northeast India.

In fact, one of the primary obstacles to development in Northeast India is the fact that after the partition of

India (in 1947) it became landlocked and thereafter with the formation of Bangladesh in 1971.The then Prime Minister Narasimha Rao wanted to take advantage of the fast-growing economies of the ASEAN region with which India already had historical ties. When PM Modi took over in India, the "Look-East Policy" was renamed as the "Act-East Policy". Since then, there have been various initiatives that have been carried out as a part of the same.

INDIA'S GROWING TIES WITH THE ASEAN

India's Republic Day celebrations, earlier in January last year, were attended by the heads of state of all the 10 ASEAN nations in an unmistakable sign of the growing bonhomie between the two sides. The ASEAN region has taken a place of pride in India's "Act-East Policy", which aims at New Delhi's re-engagement with the countries of Southeast and East Asia, where historically it has had influence.

Taken as a whole, ASEAN represents the world's third largest market, with a combined population of more than 630 million people. At the same time, governments in Northeast India are stepping on the gas, as far as economic initiatives in the region are concerned. The Global Investors' Summit, held in the Northeast state of Assam earlier in February 2018, will go a long way in encouraging foreign companies, including those from ASEAN countries, to invest in this corner of India.

In the not-too-distant future, there is a chance that the Guwahati airport in Assam would be connected to more ASEAN cities. It is already connected to Bangkok in Thailand and to Thimphu in Bhutan. In addition, Guwahati has been connected directly to Singapore through a Druk Air (Bhutanese Airlines) flight. The Assam government has also signed on to the UDAN scheme, which will subsidize carriers flying to the region in a bid to improve the air connectivity in this part of the country. There are also reports that Guwahati could be connected to five other airports besides Singapore. This is a big step forward not only for Guwahati and Assam, but for the rest of the region as well.

WHAT'S IN IT FOR ASEAN?

India is one of the fastest growing major economies in the world. It is also a young country in terms of the median age of its population, thus presenting a huge opportunity for firms from the ASEAN countries.

Engagement with India would also help the ASEAN countries develop an alternative to the Chinese model of investment. Although all ASEAN members have welcomed Beijing's One Belt One Road (OBOR) initiative, many of them still have reservations about Beijing's real intentions. For example, Myanmar has suspended the construction of the Myitsone Dam in the northern part of the country owing to concerns about the feasibility of the project and also because the majority of the electricity was to be supplied back to China. Some of the ASEAN countries are also drawing lessons from the experience of Sri Lanka, which took loans from China to construct the Hambantota port and has been heavily in debt ever since.

The China-Pakistan Economic Corridor (CPEC) is also in focus these days.

India and the ASEAN countries are also discussing the prospect of signing a RCEP or Regional Comprehensive Economic Partnership trade agreement along with a few other countries, which has assumed more significance after the United States pulled out of the Trans-Pacific Partnership (TPP).

The Delhi Declaration, issued on the occasion of the ASEAN-India Commemorative Summit earlier in January 2018 notes "the cross-cultural exchanges and civilizational linkages between Southeast Asia and India over several millennia".[1] Indeed, whether it be the Angkor Vat temple complex in Cambodia or the island of Bali in Muslim majority Indonesia or Indonesia's state philosophy of *Pancasila*, New Delhi's ties with the ASEAN countries goes back aeons ago. It was only after the opening up of the Indian economy in the early nineties and the launch of what was then called the "Look-East Policy", that things began to look up once again for India-ASEAN ties.

WHY IS INDIA "ACTING EAST"?

In his address to the East Asia Summit (EAS) in 2014 in Myanmar, PM Modi noted that "since entering office six months ago, my government has moved with a great sense of priority and speed to turn our 'Look East Policy' into 'Act East Policy'.[2]

So why is this "Act-East" policy key for India?

First, for economic reasons, India must stay connected with these parts of the world, which have some of the fastest growing economies in the world. PM Modi's government came to power riding on a huge wave of anger at the previous government as it was seen as being incapable of preventing India's economic decline. Hence, for PM Modi's government to succeed, it is important for India's economy to do well.

Second, for strategic relations, as many of these countries lie in India's immediate neighbourhood, any instability in these countries will directly impact India. For New Delhi to succeed economically it must have a peaceful environment and that has always been at the heart of India's foreign policy.

PM Modi's first visit outside the Indian subcontinent since taking over, was to Japan where he met the Japanese PM, Shinzo Abe. During this visit, the Japanese PM committed Tokyo to investing nearly $35 billion in India. Soon after the inauguration of PM Modi in May 2014, the then Australian Prime Minister Tony Abbott paid a visit to India, where the two nations inked an agreement for Australia to supply uranium to India, though New Delhi is not a signatory to the Nuclear Non-Proliferation Treaty (NPT).

New Delhi has also been helped by some fortuitous turn of events in its immediate neighbourhood. The success of the National League for Democracy (NLD) in neighbouring Myanmar made the Modi government's task easier since Myanmar is India's land bridge to the ASEAN region. PM Modi has also settled India's age-old boundary dispute with Bangladesh.

PM Modi heads a BJP-led government at home which has a commanding majority in the Lok Sabha, the lower and more powerful house of the Indian Parliament and hence his government is not prone to the pulls and pressures of coalition politics as happened during the last time when the Congress-party led motley coalition of various parties hobbled the then PM Dr Manmohan Singh's options when it came to foreign policy issues.

However, things are not all rosy in the India-ASEAN equation. There a quite a few loose ends that need to be tied since trade levels have been much lower than the actual potential. In 2016-2017, ASEAN-India trade stood at US$ 71 billion in 2016-17, which was 10.85 per cent of India's external trade. Tourism is another area that has not lived up to its potential. Although the number of outbound tourists from India to the ASEAN countries has increased, India only accounts for 3 per cent of tourist arrivals to the ASEAN region. The number of tourists from the ASEAN countries to India is nothing much to crow about.

Meanwhile, trade negotiations are at a delicate stage over the Regional Comprehensive Economic Partnership (RCEP). New Delhi has certain reservations about the RCEP while the ASEAN nations would like India to sign on to the RCEP.

It is also clear from the trends that since PM Modi took office, his government has continued from where the previous governments has left and this is indeed praiseworthy as foreign policy initiatives are mostly successful when they maintain continuity and momentum.

ASEAN will be a major engine for India's growth in the years ahead and hence it is very important that India's "Act-East Policy" continues to pick up steam. The "Act-East Policy" is also crucial for the economic development of India's Northeastern region (which has lagged behind other parts of the country in economic terms). This region serves as India's gateway to the ASEAN region[3] and hence could reap the maximum benefits of India's "Act-East" policy. At the same time, it is important for both India and ASEAN to assess the challenges plaguing their ties and work on them.

INDIAN PROJECTS IN MYANMAR

China's ambitious One Belt, One Road (OBOR) initiative has taken the world by storm and forced everyone to sit up and take notice. Most ASEAN countries have jumped on to the OBOR bandwagon, while New Delhi has opted to sit out. So, when India's Cabinet Committee on Economic Affairs gave its approval for the upgradation and widening of a section of roadway between the capital of India's Northeastern state of Manipur, Imphal, and the town of Moreh, located on the border with Myanmar, it generated some buzz in both academic and policy circles. The Asian Development Bank (ADB) has provided loan assistance for this project under the South Asian Sub-Regional Economic Cooperation (SASEC) Road Connectivity Investment Programme.

While there is nothing special on the surface of it about this go-ahead, what is worth noting here is that this section of roadway is part of the ambitious India-Myanmar-Thailand (IMT) trilateral highway, which when completed in 2020 has the potential to transform the economic landscape of this entire region. The IMT highway will connect Moreh in India's Manipur state to Mae Sot in Thailand via Myanmar.

SO, WHY IS THIS HIGHWAY CRUCIAL FOR INDIA?

First, it will help improve connectivity between India's remote Northeastern part and Southeast Asia. For long, the lack of physical connectivity with Southeast Asia has been an Achilles' Heel in India's "Act-East Policy". The trilateral highway will improve India's connectivity with Myanmar and Thailand and in the future there are plans to connect it with pre-existing roads and take it all the way to Vietnam.

Second, while construction of this road started as the India-Myanmar friendship road way back in 2001, the non-attendance by India at China's Belt and Road Forum in Beijing in 2017 seems to have injected a new measure of earnestness among Indian policy manners when it comes to executing such road projects.

Third, Northeast India has been lagging behind other parts of the country when it comes to infrastructure. In May 2017, PM Modi inaugurated India's longest river bridge over the river Lohit in the northeastern state of Assam, very close to the border with China. When completed, the IMT highway will also give easy access to the Northeastern states to the sea (via Myanmar).

Fourth, as the stand-off with China over its road-building activity in Bhutanese territory (claimed by China) in 2017 shows, Beijing is trying to improve the infrastructure in its border areas. This seems to be intended with the dual purpose of facilitating economic development and allowing quick movement of its military personnel and hardware, if needed. Hence, New Delhi's earlier strategy of not building good infrastructure in the Northeast, to deter Chinese invasion (as in 1962) obviously does not hold much ground, under the present circumstances. In the future, China has plans to build a railhead right to the doorsteps of the Indian state of Arunachal Pradesh.

WHAT'S IN IT FOR MYANMAR?

There has been domestic opposition to some Chinese projects infrastructure in Myanmar like the Myitsone dam and hence authorities in Myanmar are trying to find a balance between relying excessively on investment from China and seeking investment and technology from countries like India.

It was during the visit of former President Htin Kyaw of Myanmar to India in August 2016 that an MoU for "cooperation in the construction/upgradation of the bridges and approach road in Tamu-Kyigone-Kalewa section" and an "MoU for cooperation in the Construction/Upgradation of Kalewa-Yagyi road section of the Trilateral Highway in Myanmar" were signed.[4]

India is also involved in the Kaladan Multi Modal Transit Transport Project in Myanmar, which involves connectivity between Northeastern India and the port of Sittwe in Myanmar through the Kaladan river in Myanmar. This includes building of an integrated port and inland water transport terminal in Sittwe, dredging and development of a navigation channel along the Kaladan river from the port of Sittwe until Paletwa (in Myanmar) and thereafter building road connectivity between Paletwa to the India-Myanmar border. As and when the project is completed, goods could be transported from the Northeastern states via Sittwe to other ports in India and also to Southeast Asia via the sea route.

It is important to note here that the former President of Myanmar, U Htin Kyaw chose India as his first destination for a state visit soon after taking over as the President. During this visit, it was agreed that India would be funding the construction of 69 bridges in Myanmar.

WHY ASEAN AND INDIA ARE IMPORTANT FOR EACH OTHER?

First, India and ASEAN celebrated 25 years of their diplomatic partnership in 2017. Now, there are 30 dialogue mechanisms between India and the ASEAN, including a Summit and seven Ministerial meetings in such areas like Foreign Affairs, Commerce, Tourism, Agriculture, Environment, Renewable Energy and Telecommunications.

Second, connectivity is the key issue these days for both India and ASEAN. India is part of the India-

Myanmar-Thailand (IMT) trilateral highway, which will extend all the way from Moreh in Northeastern India to Mae Sot in Thailand.

Third, India has decided not to participate in Beijing's ambitious One-Belt One Road (OBOR) initiative (also known the Belt and Road Initiative). Although the ASEAN nations are participating in the OBOR, they would like to keep their options open with regards to connectivity initiatives emanating from India and some of them are also keen on investing in infrastructure projects within India. At the same time, it needs to be stressed here that the ASEAN member-states do not have any territorial disputes with India and New Delhi is largely seen as a benign power in the region.

The "One Belt One Road" (OBOR) initiative (also known the Belt and Road initiative) has been pushed by Chinese President Xi Jinping, who has often talked about the so-called "Chinese Dream". The OBOR is, in many ways, a re-invention of the ancient Chinese Silk Roads, which ran from China to Europe and branched off to various countries, including India. Apart from the "Maritime Silk Road", the other part of the OBOR is the "Silk Road Economic Belt," through which China is trying to build land connectivity through the Central Asian countries to Europe.

At this point, it does not seem like if India has a clear strategy to deal with China's growing maritime presence in the Indian Ocean region. New Delhi has not joined Beijing One Belt One Road (OBOR) initiative. It is also worried about Beijing's so-called "String of Pearls" strategy, under which it has already helped construct ports at Gwadar in Pakistan, Hambantota in Sri Lanka, Chittagong in Bangladesh and Kyaukpyu in Myanmar.

India reels under a huge trade deficit when it comes to bilateral trade with China and there are no signs that it might be slashed. Beijing has also stepped up its cooperation with Pakistan as in the China-Pakistan Economic Corridor (CPEC), which aims to connect Gwadar in Pakistan's Arabian Sea coast to Kashgar in the Xinjiang province of Western China. In 2017, though the total trade between India and China reached a historic high of $84.44 billion, the trade deficit has also ballooned to US$51.75 billion. However, the informal Summit at Wuhan in China in April 2018 between Indian PM Narendra Modi and Chinese President Xi Jinping seems to have the potential of rebooting the fraught ties between India and China.

Fourth, India has always been the resident power in the Indian Ocean region with the sole exception of the United States. Its Navy has had a commanding presence in the region between the Strait of Hormuz and the Strait of Malacca while its Andaman and Nicobar chain of islands lies at the entrance of the Strait of Malacca, which has been termed by many observers as China's Achilles Heel. The setting up of a tri-services command by India in the Andaman and Nicobar islands gives it an unmatched reach in the region. This is important for the ASEAN memberstates as well, many of which conduct joint naval exercises with the Indian Navy.

WHAT CAN INDIA AND ASEAN DO TOGETHER?

There a quite a few things that India and ASEAN can achieve together.

First, trade levels between India and ASEAN have been much lower than their actual potential. In 2016-2017, ASEAN-India trade stood at around US$70 billion, which was 10.85 per cent of India's external trade. India's External Affairs Minister Sushma Swaraj had noted that "the region comprising ASEAN and India together represents a combined population of 1.85 billion which is a quarter of the global population and a gross domestic product of over US$3.8 trillion, creating one of the largest economic spaces in the world."[5]

Second, tourism is another area that has not lived up to its potential. Although the number of outbound tourists from India to the ASEAN member-countries has increased, India only accounts for three per cent of tourist arrivals to the Southeast Asian region. The number of tourists from Southeast Asia to India is also nothing much to crow about. India has the potential to attract a large number of tourists from the Southeast Asian countries, especially given the Buddhist connection between the two sides. Places like Bodh Gaya and Northeast India could be of particular interest to the Southeast Asian ASEAN nations. However, in order to pluck this low-hanging fruit, New Delhi would have to further relax the visa regime for nationals from the ASEAN member-countries.

Third, trade negotiations are at a delicate stage over the Regional Comprehensive Economic Partnership

(RCEP). New Delhi has certain reservations about the RCEP while the ASEAN member-nations would like India to sign on to the RCEP. Both the sides will have to be patient with the negotiations.

Fourth, the ASEAN member-states should take advantage of India's "Act-East Policy" by engaging closely with the state governments in this part of the country. This will also help in the economic development of India's Northeastern region.

CHALLENGES

There are significant challenges in the implementation of some of the agreements, which India has signed with the various ASEAN member-countries. Projects like the Indian-funded Kaladan Multi-Modal Transport Corridor Project have run into long delays. Besides, non-traditional security threats like terrorism, piracy, people-trafficking, among others, also present significant challenges for India in the maritime arena and this is where it can cooperate with the ASEAN by sharing intelligence and resources. New Delhi has borne the brunt of terrorist attacks through the sea, as seen in the horrendous Mumbai 2008 attacks. However, coastal security remains a concern especially as India has a huge massive coastline.

In the years ahead, ASEAN will be a major engine for India's growth. Hence, at this critical juncture in ASEAN-India ties, it is important for both sides of them to reflect on the successes and the challenges in their burgeoning ties. The participation of all the ASEAN Heads of State at last year's Republic Day celebrations is both an indicator of the time-tested historical ties between India and the ASEAN, and an indicator of things to come. However, India and ASEAN should ensure that the differences on some issues should not be allowed to develop into roadblocks, lest they be caught in a quagmire of their own making.

In the field of trade, the ASEAN-India Trade in Goods Agreement was signed in 2009 and another one on ASEAN-India Trade-in-Services and Investments was inked in 2015. The growing trade between India and ASEAN is a healthy sign, especially given the winds of protectionism that are sweeping across the world, particularly in the wake of the Trump Administration taking office in the US and its walking away from treaties like the Trans-Pacific Partnership (TPP).

ASEAN-India cooperation is also very important in non-traditional security issues like human trafficking. The ASEAN countries are already reeling under the impact of the Rohingya issue (in Myanmar) which has seen its impact also in other countries in the ASEAN region. Some of these Rohingya refugees have also settled in India and hence this is a direct example of how issues in ASEAN countries impact India.

There are also plans to upgrade the Rih-Tiddim road near Myanmar's border with Mizoram. This assumes significance since a lot of unorganised trade happens through this route in Mizoram. Then there is also a huge potential for cooperation between India and ASEAN countries like Singapore, especially in the field of ports.

The ambitious Sagarmala project aims to usher in an era of port-led growth in the country, especially given India's long coastline. "As part of Sagarmala Programme, more than 577 projects, with an estimated project cost of 8.57 lakh crore, have been identified for implementation over a 20-year time period (2015-2035). This would be utilised across the areas of port modernisation and new port development, port connectivity enhancement, port-linked industrialization and coastal community development."[7]

ASEAN countries like Singapore stand to gain a lot from this initiative as they have a rich experience in both building and running ports in different parts of the world and hence its role will be crucial in the success of this key initiative of the Modi government. This will also go a long way in improving the efficiency of Indian ports, to bring it in line with international ports.

One of the mainstays of Indian foreign policy under the Modi government has been its "Act-East Policy"– which aims at India's closer engagement with Southeast Asia and East Asia. Vietnam is a key element of this policy (known earlier as the "Look-East Policy"). Hanoi is important for India's outreach efforts in the ASEAN region, besides New Delhi's plans for increasing its connectivity with the ASEAN countries. Former Vietnamese President Tran Dai Quang visited India in March last year and many items were discussed during this visit. Although Vietnam took part in China's Belt and Road Forum in May 2017, it still has concerns about Beijing's strategic motives, especially in the South China

Sea region. Vietnam disputes China's claims in the South China Sea region (along with other countries) while Beijing has objected to the Indian state-owned Oil and Natural Gas Corporation (ONGC) Videsh Limited's oil exploration activities in the South China Sea.

While India does not have any claims in the South China Sea region, the sea lanes of communication passing through the region are important for its two-way trade with Southeast Asia, East Asia and Oceania.

The visit of former Vietnamese President Tran Dai Quang to India in March last year was a good follow-up to the visit of PM Modi to Vietnam in 2016. During this visit by PM Modi, among other things, New Delhi had extended a Line of Credit of US$500 million to Vietnam to buy defence equipment. In addition, the joint statement issued on this occasion notes that "Vietnam and India, as State Parties to the UNCLOS, urged all parties to show utmost respect for the UNCLOS, which establishes the international legal order of the seas and oceans."[8] However, not everything is rosy in this burgeoning relationship. In the economic arena, there is much for the two sides to ponder over. Total trade between New Delhi and Hanoi stood at US$ 6244.92 million during April-November of the fiscal year 2016-2017, though the two sides have set a bilateral trade target of US$15 billion by 2020.[9] As compared to that, Vietnam's trade with China in 2017 stood at US$93.8 billion.[10]

In addition, the people-to-people ties between the two countries are still underdeveloped. In addition, the number of tourists from Vietnam to India and vice versa in nothing much to write about. While some reports suggest that Vietnam is interested in acquiring the BrahMos missile from India, New Delhi seems to be non-committal at the moment. Though India's ties with Vietnam has been progressing fast on all fronts, it is important for both the sides to address the challenges confronting the relationship in order for it to reach its full potential.

ASEAN-INDIA SHOULD GO THE DISTANCE

The opening of two land-border crossings between India and Myanmar at Tamu/Moreh (in Manipur) and Rihkhawdar-Zowkhawtar (in Mizoram) will go a long way in bringing India and Myanmar closer. According to a press release issued by the Indian Embassy in Yangon, Myanmar, "the landmark Land Border Crossing Agreement between India and Myanmar, signed on May 11, 2018, has been brought into effect with the simultaneous opening of international entry-exit checkpoints at the Tamu-Moreh and the Rihkhawdar-Zowkhawtar border between Myanmar and India."

It goes without saying that New Delhi must show its political heft and diplomatic acumen in order to not only finish the India-Myanmar-Thailand trilateral highway by the deadline, but also in building a world-class road. Only then, will it be able to provide an alternative to Beijing's aggressive infrastructure building activities in India's immediate neighbourhood. The trilateral highway project will not only help India build physical connectivity with the ASEAN, but also improve people-to-people contacts and increase goodwill towards New Delhi in this region. After all, as they say a "good neighbour is far better than a distant relative."

NOTES

1. Ministry of External Affairs (MEA), India, Delhi Declaration of the ASEAN-India Commemorative Summit, available at http://www.mea.gov.in/bilateral documents. htm?dtl/29386Delhi+Declaration+of+the+ASEANIndia+Commemorative+Summit+to+mark+the+25th+Anniversary+of+ASEANIndia+Dialogue+Relations accessed on December 20, 2018.
2. The Hindu, "'Look East' policy now turned into 'Act East' policy: Modi" available at http://www.thehindu.com/news/national/look-east-policy-now-turned-into-act-east-policymodi/article6595186.ece accessed on January 10, 2019.
3. Thingnam Kishan Singh (ed.) (2008). Look East Policy & India's North East: Polemics and Perspectives. New Delhi: Concept Publishing Company.
4. Ministry of External Affairs, India, India-Myanmar Joint Statement during the visit of the President of Myanmar to India available at https://www.mea.gov.in/bilateraldocuments. htm?dtl/27343/India+Myanmar+Joint+Statement+during+the+visit+of+the+President+of+Myanmar+to+India+29+August+2016 accessed on February 20, 2019.
5. Raksha Anirveda, October 2018, available at http://www.raksha-anirveda.com/wp-content/uploads/2018/10/raksha-anirveda-october-2018.pdf accessed on December 20, 2018.

6. Ministry of External Affairs, ASEAN-India relations, available at https://www.mea.gov.in/Portal/Foreign Relation/ASEAN_India_August_2017.pdf accessed on January 20, 2019.
7. The Hindu Businessline, Sagarmala: Projects worth 72,000 cr to be awarded this fiscal year available at https:// www.thehindubusinessline.com/economy/ logistics/sagarmala-projects-worth-72000-cr-to-beawarded-this-fiscal-year/article23993430.ece accessed on January 20, 2019.
8. Ministry of External Affairs, Joint Statement between India and Vietnam during the visit of Prime Minister to Vietnam, available at http://www.mea.gov.in/bilateral-documents.htm?dtl/27362 Joint+Statement+ between+ India+and+Vietnam+during+the+visit+of+ Prime+ Minister+to+Vietnam accessed on December 31, 2018.
9. Ministry of External Affairs, India, India-Vietnam Relations, available at http://www.mea.gov.in/Portal/ ForeignRelation/Vietnam_May_2017.pdf accessed on February 20, 2019.
10. Vietnam Net, Vietnam's trade surplus hits US$2.7 billion in 2017, available at http://english.vietnamnet.vn/fms/ business/193066/vietnam-s-trade-surplus-hits-us-2-7-billion-in-2017.html accessed on January 20, 2019.

3

INDIA-JAPAN TIES

I have made a number of visits to Japan. In the course of these visits, I have met many Japanese academics, journalists and others with an interest in India. One such gentleman is Takabumi Suzuoki, who worked earlier with one of the major Japanese publications–*Nikkei.* During the course of one such conversation, I asked him, what is the one thing which Japan and the Japanese value the most? His answer was simple, but it set me thinking and gave me an understanding into how the Japanese psyche works. He said it was "trust". This will be the key word in this renewed phase of engagement between India and Japan, and especially between Northeastern India and Japan. The important factor will be the delivery of key projects which have been inked between Japan and India. Since Japan is only the funding side and the executing side is India (and Indian agencies), hence the delivery of the projects will be key.

FACTORS THAT ARE BRINGING THEM CLOSER

Japan and India had close ties even in the period before India's independence when Tokyo helped revolutionaries like Subhash Chandra Bose and Rash

Behari Bose in India's struggle against colonial rule. However, the relations fizzled out in the Cold War-era as Japan became a steadfast US ally, while India became a non-aligned country.

It was only in the late 1980's that the relations began to pick up, in the aftermath of the Japanese automaker Suzuki's entry into the Indian market, where it became a runaway success. The liberalisation of the Indian economy in the early 1990's prodded more Japanese companies to enter the fledgling Indian market. However, the relations sunk to a historic low in the wake of India's nuclear tests in 1998. Japan has had a strict aversion to nuclear arms because of its past as the only country to have suffered from the impact of atomic weapons. However, the relations began to pick up after the visit of the then Japanese PM Yoshiro Mori to India in the year 2000.

The relations have never looked back ever since and the two countries now have an annual summit at the Prime Ministerial level. What is worth noting is that closer bilateral ties between Japan and India have cross-party support in both the countries. The Modi government in India has taken off from where the previous UPA-II government has left.

Japan has been involved in a big way in India's economic transformation. The maximum chunk of Japanese Official Development Assistance (ODA) has been coming to India since 2003-2004. In addition, Japan is involved in a host of big-ticket projects in India like the western dedicated freight corridor, the Delhi-Mumbai

Industrial Corridor (DMIC) and the Chennai-Bengaluru Industrial Corridor.

A Comprehensive Economic Partnership Agreement (CEPA) between Japan and India has become operational since August 2011, although trade levels are still low. India has also invited Japan to invest in its Northeast, which is a major development, as previously the Indian government has been wary of inviting other countries to invest in this part of the country due to its strategic location and security concerns.[1] Meanwhile, Japanese business interests in China have suffered on account of differences over political issues. Hence, India could well emerge as the next big destination for Japanese investments.

Both Japan and India also share concerns over China's growing belligerence in the region. While Japan is involved in a maritime dispute with China, India has a disputed land border with China and the two nations fought a limited border war in 1962. In addition, Chinese assistance to Pakistan, especially for its nuclear programme, has India worried. China's so-called "strings of pearls" strategy has seen Beijing helping out with the building of ports in Gwadar (Pakistan), Hambantota (Sri Lanka), Kyaukpyu (Myanmar) and Chittagong (Bangladesh). China's relations with Japan also are going through a rough phase, particularly in the wake of Chinese claims over the Japanese-controlled Senkaku islands. Meanwhile, China's unilateral declaration of a new Air Defence Identification Zone (ADIZ) and its aggressive acts with countries like Vietnam and the Philippines has only complicated matters.

At the same time, India's improving relations with the US have also helped bring Japan and India closer. As opposed to the Cold War era, when India was close to the erstwhile Soviet Union, the relations between India and the US have warmed up in the post-Cold War era. India has also been buying US-made military hardware which has increased the interoperability between US, Indian and Japanese forces. At the same time, Japan, India and the US have also been holding a trilateral dialogue amongst themselves since December 2011.

Japan and India are also cooperating in other forums like the East Asia Summit and in forums like the G-4 (consisting of Germany, India, Japan and Brazil) as they are trying to become permanent members of the United Nations Security Council. Besides, there are many avenues of cooperation for Japan and India in countries like Myanmar, which for New Delhi is a land bridge to the ASEAN region.

For the first time in 2012, the Japanese and the Indian navies started holding joint naval exercises. India has also invited Japan to take part in the Malabar naval exercises which were originally a bilateral naval exercise between India and the US. In addition, India is also in negotiations with Japan to buy the Shin Maywa US-2 reconnaissance aircraft . If and when this happens, it will be a momentous occasion for both India and Japan. For Japan, it will be a leap of faith especially due to the restrictions imposed by Article 9 of its constitution. Besides, the two countries are also cooperating in the exploration and production of rare-earths. For the first time, the Japanese Ground Self Defence Force personnel and the Indian Army have held joint exercises in November last year.

The lookout for the future is extremely bright for Japan-India relations. In the upcoming future, the relationship is bound to get even stronger between the two countries as they share many common values and interests.

So, how should Japan and India take their relations to the next level?

First, Japan and India should collaborate on the defence front which could include joint production of weaponry. Both Japan and India can gain from this as India is one of the world's biggest arms importers.

Second, countries like Japan, India and Vietnam need to pool their efforts and resources in order to ensure that no country becomes a hegemon in Asia. In the wake of the decrease in the power and influence of the United States in the Indo-Pacific region, this is all the more essential.

Third, maritime ties between Japan and India should be further strengthened. The Indian Navy has a commanding presence in the Indian Ocean region. The bulk of Japanese energy imports pass through the Indian Ocean and hence the Indian Navy is crucial for the safety and security of Japan's sea-lanes of communication. The Indian Navy has also been at the forefront of anti-piracy efforts in the Indian Ocean region. Hence, a treaty for collaboration between Japan and India in the maritime domain is the need of the hour.

Last, but not the least, the two countries should set up an ambitious trade target of US$50 billion in bilateral trade to be achieved by the year 2025. As of now, trade levels are still very low as compared to India-China or Japan-China trade levels.

As mentioned by Japanese PM Shinzo Abe, "the relations between Japan and India have the greatest potential of any bilateral relationship anywhere in the world."[2] Therefore, both New Delhi and Tokyo should work at strengthening the *kizuna* between the two countries.

JAPAN AND NORTHEAST INDIA

In addition, during the course of my many visits to Japan, I have found out that the terrain and the food habits are somewhat similar between Northeast India and Japan. For example, bamboo shoots are a delicacy in many parts of Northeast India and the same in Japan. In addition, many people across Northeast India eat fermented foods and the same is the case in Japan. Besides, of course, the Japanese fondness for fish is well-known and so is the case across most of Northeast India.

Meanwhile, under Japanese PM Shinzo Abe, Tokyo has adopted a pro-active stance when it comes to its foreign policy. In a meeting at the Centre for Strategic and International Studies in Washington D.C, soon after his inauguration in December 2012, PM Abe proudly announced that "Japan is back".[3]

Early into his term, he paid a visit to the controversial

Yasukuni Shrine in Tokyo, which riled Japan's immediate neighbours, China and South Korea. Under his watch, Japan has introduced new security legislation allowing for the deployment of Japanese troops outside the country even when Japan is not directly under attack. PM Abe had talked about an Asian Democratic Security Diamond which would include India, Japan, Australia and the US state of Hawaii, though it is not any closer to realisation. During the current term of Japanese PM Shinzo Abe, US-Japan relations have been further strengthened and it is no longer what Yoichi Funabashi termed as "Alliance Adrift".[4]

At the same time, India's relations with Japan have been undergoing a steady improvement. The Japanese PM was the Chief Guest at India's Republic Day celebrations in January 2014. In addition, India and Japan have also been holding a maritime affairs dialogue between them.

Bilateral cooperation between Japan and India in all fields has been increasing ever since the Cold War ended. Although India's nuclear tests of 1998 dampened the burgeoning ties, they improved dramatically in the period after August 2000 when the then Japanese PM Yoshiro Mori paid a visit to India.

There are a host of factors which are drawing Japan and India ever closer. First, both Japan and India in recent times have been faced with multiple security challenges. Among them is the growing belligerence exhibited by China, as exemplified in the deployment of advanced surface-to-air missiles in the Woody Island (referred to as

Yongxing Dao by China) in the Paracel Islands in the South China Sea. China's land-reclamation in the South China Sea is a big cause of concern and some experts have expressed the fear that in case China is able to establish a foothold in the South China Sea region, it may try to do the same in the Indian Ocean as well.

Second, India's improving ties with the US have helped to bring India and Japan closer. Japan has been a strong ally of the United States while India has been inching closer to the United States, especially after the end of the Cold War. India and the US have been conducting joint military exercises while New Delhi is also buying different kinds of military hardware from the United States, something which was almost unthinkable in the Cold War days. New Delhi now buys naval hardware from a host of countries as opposed to earlier times. India has also bought P-8 I maritime patrol aircraft from the US and is negotiating to buy Japanese-made US-2i maritime reconnaissance aircraft.

Third, Japan and India are cooperating in a wide variety of areas. They are bidding to be permanent members of the United Nations Security Council (UNSC) and have pooled their efforts along with countries like Germany and Brazil. They are also cooperating in countries like Afghanistan since Japan and India are two of the biggest international donors in Afghanistan.

Fourth, the Indian Navy is crucial for the protection of Japan's sea lanes of communication, more so since Japan is an energy deficient country. Japan's energy imports have increased after the disastrous Great East Japan Earthquake of December 2011. In the past, the Indian Navy and the Indian Coast Guard rescued a Japanese-flagged vessel MV *Alondra Rainbow* from pirates in 1999.

Fifth, New Delhi and Tokyo have concluded an agreement for "Cooperation in the Peaceful Uses of Nuclear Energy". This is more noteworthy since New Delhi has not signed either the Comprehensive Test Ban Treaty (CTBT) nor the Nuclear Non-Proliferation Treaty (NPT). India could also emerge as a big market for Japanese defence exports in the future. Prime Minister Shinzo Abe came to power in December 2012 promising to lift the Japanese economy out of its sluggishness and for the success of his so-called "Abenomics", India is of prime importance. In India too, PM Modi came to power riding on the disaffection among Indian voters with the sluggish growth of the Indian economy under the previous United Progressive Alliance (UPA) government.

Sixth, Japan and India have concluded a Comprehensive Economic Partnership Agreement (CEPA) back in 2011. Although their bilateral trade is still miniscule when compared to say India's trade with China or Japan's trade with China, there is a lot of potential for Japan-India trade levels to increase.

India is also an attractive destination for Japanese investment. New Delhi has already started the construction of a high speed railway corridor between Mumbai and Ahmedabad in India. Japan had earlier lost out to China for the introduction of a similar high-speed railway system between Jakarta and Bandung in Indonesia.

India was the first recipient of Japanese Official Development Assistance (ODA) way back in 1958, which has played an instrumental role in ensuring India's infrastructural development. Many major infrastructure development projects in India like the Delhi Metro, the Delhi-Mumbai Industrial Corridor (DMIC) and the Chennai-Bengaluru Industrial Corridor have benefitted to a huge extent from Japanese ODA.

PM Abe's grandfather, Nobusuke Kishi had visited India way back in 1957 and he had always held India in high esteem. In a major gesture from Japan, the Japanese Emperor and Empress had visited India in late 2013. This shows that the commitment to the ties exists at the highest levels in both India and Japan. PM Modi had visited Japan while he was the Chief Minister of the Indian province of Gujarat and has a long contact with Japan.

India should be wary of getting entangled in China's Maritime Silk Road since it could be a smokescreen for China to reach out to countries in India's immediate neighbourhood. Beijing's growing economy is hungry for energy resources especially from the Middle East and Africa and the Maritime Silk Road could be yet another way for China to make these countries, especially the ones in Africa even more dependent on imports from China.

Instead, New Delhi should think of its own initiative similar to the Maritime Silk Road as traditionally Indian influence has spread by the sea. India's "Act-East" policy gels well with the US' "pivot to the Asia-Pacific" and Japan's "Free and Open Indo-Pacific Strategy". India has signed a "logistics support agreement" (or LEMOA[6] in technical terms) with the US, which will allow the militaries of the two countries to use each others' bases for refuelling and logistics. This is a big leap forward from the days when India and the United States were on opposite sides of the Cold War divide, which meant that India was closer to the erstwhile Soviet Union.

Much water has flowed down the mighty Ganges since the end of the Cold War. That was when Japan and India started coming closer to each other–again–notwithstanding the dip in their ties in the wake of India's nuclear tests in 1998.

In spite of historical ties dating back eons ago, the two countries drifted apart in the period after India's independence in 1947, as New Delhi inched closer to the erstwhile Soviet Union, while Japan became an ally of the United States.

It was only after the end of the Cold War and the dissolution of the Soviet Union that the two countries decided to re-imagine their ties in the wake of the changed geopolitical realities.

Now, Tokyo is one of the biggest foreign investors in India, and New Delhi has been the biggest recipient of Japanese Official Development Assistance since 2003. The fact that the India is one of the fastest growing economies in the world has generated huge interest from Japan and Japanese companies, which are keen on exploring big markets like India.

Meanwhile, India urgently needs to shore up its infrastructure sector, and Japan's help is key in this area. Tokyo has provided financial and technical know-how for many big-ticket infrastructure projects in India, like the Delhi Metro project, the Delhi-Mumbai Industrial Corridor (DMIC), the Western Dedicated Freight Corridor, and the Chennai-Bangalore Industrial Corridor (CBIC). In addition, during his visit to India in September 2017, Japanese Prime Minister Shinzo Abe laid the foundation stone for the construction of the India's first high-speed railway corridor between Mumbai and Ahmedabad.

The two countries are cooperating in the Indian energy sector. They signed a civilian nuclear deal during the visit of Indian Prime Minister Narendra Modi to Japan in November 2016 that has now come into force. It is designed to address the issue of perennial energy shortage in India. Access to adequate energy resources will be *sine qua non* for India's continued growth at present levels. Then there is the issue of worsening pollution in India as it rapidly develops, and here too Japan can help India cut down on its pollution levels with its high-end green technologies.

In addition, there is a huge potential for cooperation between the two countries in the defence sector, especially as India is one of the world's biggest defence importers. India and Japan now hold joint naval exercises (called JIMEX), which are a far cry from the earlier times when there were only exercises involving the coast guard of the two nations. PM Modi has outlined his intention to increase the indigenization of India's defence manufacturing sector and Japan can be a very competent partner in the same.

India's improving ties with the U.S. have also played a role in its improving ties with Japan. The three nations are now part of the annual *Malabar* naval exercise. *Malabar* actually started as an annual naval exercise between India and the United States back in 1992.

The close personal chemistry between the two prime ministers is another factor bringing the two countries closer. After PM Modi took office in May 2014, the first bilateral visit he paid outside of the Indian sub-continent was to Japan, clearly indicating the foreign policy priorities of his administration. As evident in the Indian government's decision to allow Japan to participate in building infrastructure in India's northeastern region, where previously other foreign countries have not been allowed to invest, New Delhi has signalled that it is willing to trust Japan.

JAPANESE INVESTMENT IN NORTHEAST INDIA

New Delhi has welcomed Japanese involvement in the region. During the visit of Japanese PM Shinzo Abe to India in September 2017, the two countries "welcomed the India-Japan cooperation on development of India's North Eastern Region (NER) as a concrete symbol of developing synergies between India's "Act East Policy" and Japan's "Free and Open Indo Pacific Strategy."[7]

In May 2017, when Chinese President Xi Jinping formally announced his Belt and Road Initiative (BRI) in Beijing, India did not take part in the same, owing to sovereignty issues. Hence, it becomes all the more important for New Delhi to step up its physical connectivity with the ASEAN region and with Japan. Northeast India's location is key to these efforts, more so as India celebrated 25 years of its dialogue partnership with ASEAN in 2017.

With the term "Indo-Pacific" gaining increasing currency worldwide in both scholarly and official circles, New Delhi's foreign policy moves are being watched (and analysed) with interest across the world, especially in Asia. At the same time, countries across the world (especially in Asia) are adjusting to the rise of China. The ASEAN nations are no different. Many of them have huge amounts of trade with China, while at the same time being embroiled in territorial disputes with Beijing. No wonder they are looking at increasing their foreign policy options and the rise of India has given them this option.

China's ambitious One Belt, One Road (OBOR) initiative has taken the world by storm and forced everyone to sit up and take notice. Most Asian countries have jumped on to the OBOR bandwagon, while New Delhi has opted to sit out.

One of the important facets of New Delhi's growing ties with Tokyo has been the burgeoning cooperation between the "Land of the Rising Sun" and India's Northeast (which incidentally sees the earliest sunrise in

India). Japan would be financing the almost 20-km Dhubri-Phulbari bridge in Northeast India. When completed, it will become India's longest bridge, surpassing the Bhupen Hazarika Setu in Assam, which is 9.15 kms across.[8]

Northeast India has lagged behind many other parts of the country in terms of development. However, India's "Act-East Policy" (known earlier as the "Look-East Policy") has come as a harbinger of hope for the Northeast, especially as New Delhi has increased its engagement with countries in the ASEAN region and with countries like Japan.

MAJOR JAPANESE INITIATIVES IN NORTHEAST INDIA

Under PM Abe, Japan has embarked on the "Free and Open Indo-Pacific Strategy" which aims at "promoting connectivity between Asia, the Middle East and Africa." It actually builds on PM Abe's landmark speech before the Indian Parliament in August 2007 (during his earlier term in office) titled "Confluence of the Two Seas" where he noted that "the Pacific and the Indian Oceans are now bringing about a dynamic coupling as seas of freedom and of prosperity. A "broader Asia" that broke away geographical boundaries is now beginning to take on a distinct form."[9]

Japan has a historical connect with the northeastern part of India, dating back to World War II. In the light of China's OBOR (One Belt One Road) initiative, Japan is trying in its own way to increase its presence in the infrastructure sector in Asia and across the world with initiatives like the "Partnership for Quality Infrastructure". Tokyo has already been closely involved economically in ASEAN countries like Myanmar.

With regards to Northeast India, Japan has contributed Official Development Assistance (ODA) loans for the North East Road Network Connectivity Improvement Project and will extend a loan to the tune of approximately Rs 2239 crore.[10] This encompasses the National Highways 54 in Mizoram and National Highways 40 and 51 which pass through the state of Meghalaya in Northeastern India. Tokyo is also supporting the construction of a new bridge in Dawki, which links Meghalaya and Bangladesh and this new bridge will replace the existing 90-year old bridge.

Skill development is another area of cooperation between Japan and NE India. In the future, more youths from the Northeastern part of India might be able to take advantage of programmes like the Technical Intern Training Programme (TTIP), which trains people in areas like day care for elderly people, given Japan's growing elderly population.

Sports could be another area of cooperation since sportspersons from Northeast India have excelled themselves both on the national and international stage. This is significant since Tokyo will be hosting the Olympics and the Paralympics in 2020. Tokyo is considering cooperation with the Manipur National Sports University.

During a visit to Meghalaya, the Japanese Ambassador to India, noted that "the North East assumes critical importance in our bilateral relationship and the region should benefit more from the ever-deepening partnership between Japan and India. There is a growing momentum to boost Japan-India cooperation in the North Eastern Region. Our historical ties and future-oriented views of the people are now precious asset to expand friendship between Japan and the North East.[11]

WHY IS JAPAN INTERESTED IN NORTHEAST INDIA AND WHAT LIES AHEAD?

Japan is deeply involved in Myanmar and Bangladesh and Northeast India seems like the missing link. In addition, in the light of the fact that Japan has its own "Partnership for Quality Infrastructure" initiative, this is crucial for Tokyo.

The slew of infrastructure projects being undertaken by Japan and India in the Northeastern region of India is a clear indicator of the growing bonhomie between the two countries. The fact that Japan has been allowed to invest in the strategically important Northeastern region points to the growing trust-levels between the two countries. Tokyo has already been providing ODA to India since 1958 and is India's biggest bilateral donor.

Japan's financial help will give a much-needed boost to India's "Act-East Policy" and speed up New Delhi's engagement, not only with Japan, but also with the ASEAN region and could very well be a game-changer as far as infrastructure development in Northeast India is concerned. It will also be yet another shot-in-the-arm for what Japanese PM Shinzo Abe has described as the relationship with the "greatest potential of any bilateral relationship in the world".[12]

Japan and India concluded a Special Strategic and Global Partnership during the visit by Prime Minister Modi to Japan in 2014. On the other hand, Modi chose Japan as his first foreign destination for a bilateral visit beyond the Indian subcontinent, clearly laying out the foreign policy priorities of his government.

The two prime ministers have invested a lot of energy and personal capital in the relationship. After the Modi government took office, the "Look-East Policy" was renamed the "Act-East Policy." The "Act-East Policy" aims to reinvigorate New Delhi's historical engagement with countries in Southeast Asia and East Asia. At the same time, Tokyo has embarked on its "Free and Open Indo-Pacific strategy".

However, of late, there seem to be some differences between India and Japan with regards to Beijing's Belt and Road Initiative (BRI) or the so-called One Belt One Road (OBOR). While Japan has signalled that is willing to cooperate with China on a case-by-case basis on the BRI, India has affirmed its staunch disapproval of the initiative, because of concerns over sovereignty and transparency, among others.

WHAT CAN INDIA DO FOR JAPAN?

First, open sea lanes of communication heading in and out of Japan are critical for the health of its economy. India has a huge naval presence in the Indian Ocean region and hence is a key player in Japan's "Free and Open Indo-Pacific Strategy". The two countries now conduct annual bilateral naval exercises called the JIMEX, which are a far cry from the times when they only had exercises at the coast guard level. India, Japan and the U.S. are also part of the *Malabar* trilateral exercises, where Japan was included as a permanent member in 2015.

Second, India and Japan seem to be keen on collaborating in third countries like Sri Lanka. China has already taken the Hambantota port in Sri Lanka on lease, and is also engaged in several other projects in the island.

Third, India is also spreading its wings in its neighbourhood by investing heavily in the development of the Chabahar port in Iran. It does not lie very far from the Gwadar port in Pakistan, which China has helped to construct. In the future, Japan could also think about collaborating with India in Iran's Chabahar port.

Fourth, on the international stage, India, Japan, the U.S., and Australia have formed the "new quad." In September 2017, Sushwa Swaraj, Japanese Foreign Minister Taro Kono, and the former U.S. Secretary of State Rex Tillerson met on the sidelines of the United Nations General Assembly, where they agreed to work together on strategically important ports and other infrastructure in the Indo-Pacific region, among other things.

The two countries also discussed cooperation in new areas, like skills development, Japanese language training in India, and the possibility of Indian professionals working in Japan under the Technical Intern Training Program.

There is growing complementarity between India's "Act-East Policy" and Japan's "Free and Open Indo-Pacific Strategy". In addition, both countries are faced with a rising China on the one hand and turbulence in their immediate neighbourhoods on the other.

THE CHANGED REALITIES IN THE INDO-PACIFIC

Of late, the term "Indo-Pacific" has gained increasing currency, especially under President Donald Trump. India's importance in the US foreign policy calculus has been increasing progressively, as seen in a major policy speech delivered by the former US Secretary of State Rex Tillerson. He remarked that "the United States and India are increasingly global partners with growing strategic convergence."[13]

For starters, it encapsulates the growing importance of India and the Indian Ocean countries, especially as Beijing seeks to carve out its own sphere of influence in the region and beyond.

With the US walking out of agreements like the Trans-Pacific Partnership (TPP), many Asian countries and others are beginning to wonder if Washington is really serious about performing its traditional role of ensuring a rules-based order in Asia.

In addition, contrary to the fiery rhetoric used by Trump in his election campaign, during his visit to China in November 2017, he seemed to be bowled over by the majestic reception, which his Chinese hosts had arranged. In addition, President Trump has been running with the hares and hunting with the hounds with regards to China. He needs Beijing's help when it comes to tackling Pyongyang's provocative shenanigans.

Chinese President Xi Jinping has also strengthened his hold on power. At the Party Congress in October 2017, he was given a second consecutive five-year term. Meanwhile, countries like Australia have been debating the extent of Chinese influence in the country, and the Trump administration's vacillations have not done much to assuage growing concerns in Canberra.

New Delhi, on the other hand, has had a run-in with the Dragon in 2017, when China started constructing a road through the Doklam region of Bhutan (claimed by China). Though the standoff ended much sooner than most in Delhi would have expected, it may just be the ominous beginning of a new round of tensions in the region between the two Asian behemoths.

Australia's 2017 foreign policy white paper notes: "Australia is particularly concerned by the unprecedented pace and scale of China's activities. Australia opposes the use of disputed features and artificial structures in the South China Sea for military purposes."[14]

As shown by the November 2017 meeting of some senior officials from India, Japan, the US, and Australia on the sidelines of the recent ASEAN Summit and the East Asia Summit in Manila (which led to the re-establishment of the "Quad"), these countries are looking to have a countervailing structure in the region. However, the major challenge for these countries would be how to mesh their economic and strategic priorities as all of them have huge amounts of trade with China.

The revival of the "Quad" is also a step in that direction, which Japan has been actively promoting. The Japanese government has been promoting the concept of "Free and Open Indo-Pacific," which is important for its continued economic success and also for its strategic interests.

As the concept of Indo-Pacific gains increasing salience in both academic and policy circles, one must keep in mind the role of Japan and PM Abe in being one of the primary drivers of this concept and also in being far ahead of the times.

PM Abe's visit to India in September 2017 came at a time when a series of factors brought Tokyo and New Delhi closer together in a manner like never before. Both countries faced a deteriorating security environment. The "hydrogen-bomb" test by North Korea and its earlier test flight of a missile in 2017, which flew over the northern Japanese island of Hokkaido, had fuelled significant security concerns in Tokyo. Earlier, Abe had also re-jigged his Cabinet, though this was due to domestic political considerations.

Meanwhile, Beijing's aggressive moves in India's immediate neighbourhood have worried observers in New Delhi. In the stand-off with China over Doklam in Bhutan, (which is claimed by China), Japan threw its weight behind India when its ambassador to India remarked that "there should be no attempt to change the status quo on the ground by force."[15] Though both China and India have since agreed to pull back troops from Doklam, tensions persist.

India's huge population and growing economy have caught the attention of Japan Inc., especially in the light of falling demand at home and its political tensions with China. The infrastructure sector has seen wide-ranging cooperation between the two countries. Japanese financial and technical knowhow are being used in signature projects like the Delhi Metro, the Delhi-Mumbai Industrial Corridor, and the Chennai-Bangalore Industrial Corridor. It is worth noting that the biggest chunk of Japan's Official Development Assistance has been coming to India since the fiscal year 2003-2004, and it had not shrunk even during the Fukushima disaster in Japan in 2011.

Meanwhile, India's growing ties with the United States have brought it closer to steadfast US allies, like Japan. The turnaround in the ties between the world's oldest democracy and the world's most populous democracy happened after the visit of then-US President Bill Clinton to India in 2000. Since then, Indo-US relations have moved at a very fast pace, especially after the signing of the US-India civilian nuclear deal.

In the meantime, India's relations with other US allies, like Australia, also seem to be improving. Australia has also signed a civilian nuclear deal with India. Canberra has the world's largest explored uranium deposits, which is critical for the success of India's nuclear energy programme. In the past, Australia had refused to sign a civilian nuclear deal with India unless the latter acceded to the Nuclear Non-Proliferation Treaty (NPT), but things have changed now.

There have also been many others areas of cooperation between India, Japan, Australia, and the US. These four countries launched the "Quadrilateral Initiative" in 2007, though it suffered a swift death because of concerns expressed by China, in a classic instance of throwing the baby out with the bathwater. These four countries had also pooled their efforts in the wake of the devastating Indian Ocean tsunami in December 2004.

In addition, Indian Prime Minister Narendra Modi and Japan's Abe seem to have struck a close friendship. Then, there is cross-party support for close ties with Japan cutting across the political spectrum in India. Though India-Japan relations started improving after the launch of the "Look-East Policy" under the Congress government, it was carried ahead by the BJP-led NDA government. In fact, it was BJP's Atal Behari Vajpayee who was the prime minister during the visit of then-PM Yoshiro Mori of Japan, when the relations made a comeback after the chill in the wake of India's nuclear tests of 1998. Similarly, in Japan, even with the frequent change of prime ministers (until December 2012), the bilateral relationship has not suffered.

Japan was one of the countries which provided tremendous help to India during the balance of payments crisis of 1991. The relations between Asia's biggest democracy and its richest, nosedived in the wake of India's nuclear tests in 1998 when Japan imposed severe sanctions on India. However, the ties started to rebound in the wake of the visit of the then Japanese PM Yoshiro Mori to India. Since then, the relations have never looked back, especially since PM Abe took office in December 2012.

PM Abe's affection for India is well-known. During one of his visits to India, he had visited the grandson of Radha Binod Pal, the only judge who had spoken out in favour of the Japanese during the Tokyo Trials of the post-Second World War. The Japanese still revere India and in fact, the Yasukuni Shrine, in the heart of Tokyo, still houses a memorial to Justice Radha Binod Pal. It is this very Yasukuni Shrine which has roused emotions in some East Asian countries in the past whenever Japanese leaders have visited it.

INDIA, JAPAN AND SRI LANKA

Since aeons ago, Sri Lanka's strategic location has elicited the interest of a range of colonial powers ranging from the Portuguese, the Dutch, and the English, who attempted to wrest control of the "teardrop island." After its independence from British Rule in 1948, it was plagued by civil strife from 1983 until 2009. Since then, Sri Lanka has enjoyed relative stability.

However, its strategic location has meant that various countries have been trying to raise their profile in the island nation. Of late, China has pumped in a huge deal of money into the island nation. Under the previous Rajapaksa regime, Beijing invested heavily in the infrastructure sector in Sri Lanka, especially in projects like the Hambantota port, the nearby Mattala Rajapaksa International Airport, and a brand new city which is coming up off the coast of Colombo on reclaimed land.

INDIA'S ROLE AND INTEREST IN SRI LANKA

While India has had historical ties with Sri Lanka, its involvement in the Sri Lankan civil war with the sending of peacekeepers led to a lot of heartburn on both sides. However, the bilateral relations recovered thereafter, though the Rajapaksa government showed a clear tilt towards Beijing. New Delhi has seen Beijing wading into its own backyard with the so-called "String of Pearls" strategy of helping build ports in India's immediate neighborhood. Things, however, fell back into place (in some measure only) for New Delhi with Maithripala Sirisena being elected as president in January 2015.

India was initially offered the project to build a port at Hambantota by Sri Lanka, and when it dithered on the same, China moved in very fast. While New Delhi's concerns have been justified since Hambantota has suffered huge losses, on the flip side, it has meant that China has seized a strategic advantage in the island nation.

However, now New Delhi has realized that it was outwitted by Beijing in Sri Lanka and is rapidly making amends. It is also pooling in its efforts with countries like Japan as can be seen in the agreement for the setting up of a $250 million LNG-facility at Kerawalapitiya on Sri Lanka's west coast.

During the visit of the Sri Lankan PM to India in late-April 2017, a memorandum of understanding on cooperation in economic projects was signed. It envisages the joint development of the upper oil tank farm in Trincomalee by India and Sri Lanka, besides the development of a port, petroleum refinery, and other industries in Trincomalee. The MoU also provides for the development of road segments with Indian investment.

JAPAN'S INTEREST IN SRI LANKA

Japan has also had close ties with Sri Lanka in the past. During the visit of the Sri Lankan prime minister to Japan earlier in April 2017, Tokyo agreed to provide one billion yen for the "enhancement of Trincomalee Port." During the same visit, Sri Lankan Prime Minister Ranil Wickremesinghe also "endorsed Japan's Free and Open Indo-Pacific Strategy."

Japan has a growing maritime relationship with Sri Lanka. The Japanese helicopter carrier *JS Izumo* paid a goodwill visit to Sri Lanka between July 20 and July 23, 2017, after participating in the *Malabar* naval exercises between India, Japan, and the United States. The first Sri Lanka-Japan dialogue on maritime security, safety and oceanic issues was held in January 2016 in Colombo, and Tokyo announced that it would be providing two patrol vessels to Sri Lanka.

So, why should New Delhi and Tokyo join hands in Sri Lanka?

First, Japan has a Self-Defense Force (SDF) base in

Djibouti, and now China also has one. Hence, the location of Sri Lanka will be key as it lies almost halfway between the strategically crucial Straits of Malacca and the energy-rich Gulf region. As Japan is an energy-importing nation, the safety of its key sea lanes of communication is critical for the health of its economy.

Second, Sri Lanka is reeling under a huge foreign debt problem. Japan and India can help offset this debt trap issue faced by Sri Lanka and in the process earn goodwill among both the Sri Lankan government and the ordinary populace.

Third, India has close historical and ethnic ties with Sri Lanka, especially in the Tamil-dominated areas. Japan can benefit by collaborating with India in these areas, as in Trincomalee, while India and Sri Lanka can benefit from Japan's technical expertise. Although Sri Lanka has opted to join China's "One Road, One Belt" initiative, at the same time it has kept its options open with regards to countries like India and Japan. During the Sri Lankan Prime Minister's visit to Japan earlier in 2017, the two leaders "reaffirmed the importance of open, transparent and commercial use of port facilities under full Sri Lankan Government control."[16] This assumes significance in the light of concerns expressed by many countries regarding the Beijing-backed Hambantota project.

THE CHURNING WATERS IN THE INDO-PACIFIC

Both India and Japan have been reeling under Beijing's growing aggressiveness in the South China Sea region, around the Japanese-controlled Senkakus, in the

Himalayan border, and the wider Indian Ocean region. New Delhi and Tokyo should pool their efforts in Sri Lanka as not doing so may allow Beijing to seize the initiative in a country whose location makes it an indispensible part of both India's plans to maintain its prominence in the Indian Ocean region and Japan's Free and Open Indo-Pacific Strategy.

PM Abe has been a vocal proponent of what is termed as the "Asian Democratic Security Diamond" which would include Japan, India, Australia and the American state of Hawaii.[1] India has also invited Japan to invest in its Northeast, a no-go area for most other countries given its strategic location. Since India is increasing its connectivity with the rest of Southeast Asia, through projects like the India-Myanmar-Thailand trilateral highway, there will be many opportunities for Japan and India to work together in Southeast Asia.

For Japanese companies, India is an attractive market, especially since political tensions with China have also impacted Japanese businesses in China. The floods in Thailand in 2011 have not made it any less easy for Japanese companies in Thailand.

THE ROAD AHEAD

Tokyo is an important partner in India's "Act-East Policy," which aims to strengthen India's historical ties with the countries of Southeast Asia and East Asia. India is also paying renewed attention to the maritime realm as it is hobbled by a lack of options on land. Similarly, Japan is looking out not only to the Pacific Ocean, but also to the Indian Ocean as the term "Indo-Pacific" increasingly gains currency. In addition, with the Trump administration pulling the U.S. out of the Trans-Pacific Partnership (TPP), Japan has been looking out for alternative markets and India fits the bill perfectly.

Japan's strengths are high-end technology and capital, while India has highly qualified manpower and a huge market. As Japan's population shrinks and Japanese companies look for emerging markets, the Japan-India match is just right.

The view seems to be shared from the Indian side. In a speech in 2017, former Indian Foreign Secretary Dr. Jaishankar remarked: "Gradually and steadily, Japan has emerged as a special strategic partner with whom India increasingly shares a global agenda. The planned Shinkansen high-speed rail project is the symbol of these changes. But they do reflect a much more profound shift underway, one that involves a significant Japanese commitment to infrastructure modernization in India, a substantially larger investment footprint and the accompanying eco-system that nurtures these processes."

Hence, given their shared interests, it is no surprise that New Delhi and Tokyo are moving ever closer.

NOTES

1. Indrani Bagchi, "Japan enters where China is barred–northeast India" available at http://timesofindia.indiatimes.com/india/Japan-enters-where-China-is-

barrednortheast-India/articleshow/29427619.cms accessed on January 7, 2019.

2. Media Statements of Prime Minister Dr. Manmohan Singh and Prime Minister of Japan Shinzo Abe at the press event held after the annual India-Japan summit level meeting available at http://mea.gov.in/media-briefings.htm?dtl/22782Media+Statements+of+Prime+Minister+Dr+Manmohan+Singh+and+Prime+Minister+of+Japan+Shinzo+Abe+at+the+press+event+held+after+the+annual+IndiaJapan+summit+level+meeting accessed on January 10, 2019.
3. Ministry of Foreign Affairs, Japan(2013), Japan is Back, Shinzo Abe, Prime Minister of Japan, available at http://www.mofa.go.jp/announce/pm/abe/us_ 20130222en.html accessed on August 19, 2018.
4. Yoichi Funabashi (1999), Alliance Adrift (New York: Council on Foreign Relations).
5. Ministry of External Affairs (2015), India-Japan relations available at http://www.mea.gov.in/Portal/Foreign Relation/Japan_2015_07_23.pdf accessed on September 17, 2018.
6. The Hindu, New Delhi and Washington agree on logisticssupport pact, available at http://www.thehindu.com/news/national/india-us-agree-on-logistics-agreement-to-be-signedin-a-month/article8466689.ece accessed on February 21, 2019.
7. Ministry of External Affairs (India), India-Japan Joint Statement during visit of Prime Minister of Japan to India, http://www.mea.gov.in/bilateral-documents.htm?dtl/28946/IndiaJapan+Joint+Statement+during+visit+of+Prime+Minister+of+Japan+to+India+September+ 14+2017 accessed on December 9, 2018.

8. The Assam Tribune, Dhubri-Phulbari bridge work likelyto be awarded this year, available at http://www.assamtribune.com/scripts/detailsnew.asp?id=jun2118/at062, accessed on June 27, 2018.

9. Ministry of Foreign Affairs of Japan, "Confluence of the Two Seas", available at https://www.mofa.go.jp/region/asiapaci/pmv0708/speech-2.html accessed on June 29, 2018.

10. The Economic Times, Japan teams up with India forNortheast, to extend Rs 2239-crore loans available at https://economictimes.indiatimes.com/news/economy/infrastructure/japan-teams-up-with-india-for-northeast-toextend-rs-2239-crore-loans/articleshow/60703906.cms accessed on February 19, 2019.

11. Embassy of Japan in India, Address by Ambassador Hiramatsu "India, Japan and North East" 7 May 2018, available at https://www.in.emb-japan.go.jp/files/000361834.pdf accessed on February 21, 2019.

12. The Hindu, India-Japan bilateral relationship hasgreatest potential: Abe, available at https://www.thehindu.com/news/international/indiajapanbilateral-relationship-has-greatest-potential-abe/article7904075.ece accessed on June 30, 2018.

13. US Embassy in India, Secretary of State Rex Tillerson on "Defining Our Relationship with India for the Next Century", available at https://in.usembassy.gov/secretarystate-rex-tillerson-defining-relationship-india-next-century/ accessed on February 19, 2019.

14. Nikkei Asian Review, Australia hedges bets on US in foreign-policy balancing act, available at https://asia.nikkei.com/Politics/Australia-hedges-bets-on-US-

inforeign-policy-balancing-act2 accessed on February 21, 2019.

15. Times of India, Doklam stand-off: Japan backs India, says no one should try to change status quo by force, available at https://timesofindia.indiatimes.com/india/doklam-standoff-japan-backs-india-says-no-one-should-try-to-changestatus-quo-by-force/articleshow/60111396.cms accessed on January 27, 2019.
16. Ministry of Foreign Affairs, Japan, Japan-Sri Lanka Summit Meeting available at https://www.mofa.go.jp/s_sa/sw/lk/page4e_000597.html accessed on February 15, 2019.
17. Abe, Shinzo (2012), Asia's Democratic Security Diamond, http://www.project-syndicate.org/commentary/a-strategicalliance-for-japan-and-india-by-shinzo-abe accessed on July 23, 2018.

4

IMPORTANCE OF THE MARITIME DOMAIN IN JAPAN-INDIA-ASEAN TIES

"Birds of a feather flock together." This adage could very well surmise the growing collaboration between India, Japan and the ASEAN countries in the maritime realm. This comes against the backdrop of the shifting sands of geopolitics in the wider Indo-Pacific region. Even as US President Donald Trump met the North Korean strongman Kim Jong-un in Singapore in June last year and again in Hanoi earlier this year, at the same time, the US and China (the world's two biggest economies) are in the midst of a trade war.

This flux has also extended to the maritime domain. In a landmark move, the US Pacific Command has been renamed as the US Indo-Pacific Command. While India has been reaching out to Southeast Asia and East Asia through its "Act-East Policy", its maritime focus has been consistently growing. At the same time, Japan, under PM Abe, has launched its "Free and Open Indo-Pacific Strategy." The three countries already have a trilateral strategic dialogue, which has been taking place among them since December 2011.

India's Naval Doctrine of 2015 notes that the Indian Ocean accounts for "two-thirds of the world's oil shipments, one-third of bulk cargo traffic and half the world's container shipments."[1] Hence, the Indian Navy's role is very crucial in this region. Besides, it is worth noting that countries in the Indian Ocean region also face the danger of piracy and maritime terrorism. In the case of the horrendous Mumbai terrorist attacks of November 2008, the attackers came by the sea route.

Hence, it is no surprise that these three countries have pooled together in the Malabar naval exercises which actually started out as bilateral exercises between India and the US back in 1992. Japan became a permanent member of these exercises only in 2015.

In the last edition of the *Malabar* exercises (held in June 2018), the Indian Navy was represented by "two indigenously designed and built ships, the multi-purpose stealth frigate INS Sahyadri and Anti-Submarine Warfare corvette, INS Kamorta, Fleet Tanker INS Shakti and Long Range Maritime Patrol Aircraft P8I." However, India's aircraft carrier *INS Vikramaditya* was not a part of the exercises as it was undergoing a pre-scheduled refit.

The JMSDF sent a Hyuga-class helicopter carrier JS Ise with integral helicopters, the Takanami-class destroyer JS Suzunami, Akizuki class destroyer JS Fuyuzuki, two P1 Maritime Patrol Aircraft besides a submarine. The US Navy was represented by the Nimitz-class aircraft carrier, USS Ronald Reagan with its air wing, two Ticonderoga class cruisers, two Arleigh Burke class destroyers, a Los

Angeles class attack submarine and one Long Range Maritime Patrol Aircraft P8A. The exercises were conducted in two phases–the harbour phase– from June 7-10 and the sea phase from June 11-16, 2018.

A US Navy Press Release about these exercises notes that "Indian, Japanese and U.S. maritime forces have a common understanding and knowledge of a shared working environment at sea. Each iteration of this exercise helps to advance the level of understanding between the nations' sailors as members of Indo-Pacific nations, and the hope is to be able to continue this process over time to strengthen bonds and personal relationships."[2]

WHY MALABAR 2018 WAS IMPORTANT?

These exercises were important for a host of reasons.

For one, the Indo-Pacific has acquired increasing relevance under the Trump Administration in the US, the Modi administration in India and the Abe administration in Japan. Malabar 2018 was held against the backdrop of the Indian PM Narendra Modi's visit to Wuhan in China for an informal summit with the Chinese President and his keynote speech at the Shangri-La Dialogue in Singapore where he noted that "oceans had an important place in Indian thinking since pre-Vedic times. Thousands of years ago, the Indus Valley Civilisation as well as Indian peninsula had maritime trade."[3]

Very early on in his term in March 2015, during a visit to Mauritius, Seychelles and Sri Lanka, PM Modi had noted that "we seek a future for Indian Ocean that lives up to the name of SAGAR – Security and Growth for All in the Region."[4] New Delhi is also worried about China's so-called "string of pearls" strategy which has seen Beijing help build ports and port-related infrastructure in Gwadar (Pakistan), Hambantota (Sri Lanka), Kyaukpyu (Myanmar) and Chittagong (Bangladesh).

Second, the US has also advocated a stronger line on China during last year's Shangri-La Dialogue and had disinvited the Chinese Navy from the RIMPAC exercises. Former US Defense Secretary Mattis had noted at the Shangri-La Dialogue 2018 that "as initial response to China's continued militarization of the South China Sea, last week we disinvited the People's Liberation Army Navy from the 2018 Rim of the Pacific Exercise, as China's behavior is inconsistent with the principles and the purposes of the RIMPAC exercise, the world's largest Naval exercise".[5]

Third, Tokyo, as part of its "Free and Open Indo-Pacific Strategy" would not want itself to be boxed in by China given that it depends on free and open sea-lanes of communication in the wider Indo-Pacific region for both its energy imports and also for its exports. In addition, Beijing claims the Senkakus (which are controlled by Japan) and known as Diaoyu in China.

Fourth, India's relations with both the US and Japan have been improving steadily. New Delhi has signed the Logistics Exchange Memorandum of Agreement (LEMOA) with the US, which allows the US and India to use designated bases in each others' countries for refuelling and replenishment. In addition, Japan and India have also been holding joint naval exercises known as the JIMEX since 2012, which is very different from the times when the two countries would conduct joint exercises only at the coast guard level. India is now buying a wide-range of weapons from the US as opposed to the earlier times when the former Soviet Union (and its successor state Russia) used to be almost the only supplier of weapons to India. It is noteworthy that arms imports by India from the US rose by a staggering 550 per cent during 2013-2017 as opposed to the previous five years.

Fifth, the Malabar exercises build on the growing cooperation between these countries (and Australia) in the maritime arena, which first took effect after the disastrous Indian Ocean Tsunami of December 2004. In addition, India has also decided to base fighter jets in the strategically important Andaman and Nicobar islands, giving it an even greater reach in the wider Indian Ocean region. New Delhi is also looking to develop the Sabang port in Indonesia, which lies very close to India's Andaman and Nicobar group of islands.New Delhi is also building its first home-grown aircraft carrier, which is expected to be ready by late 2020.

ROUGH WATERS AHEAD

While it is clear that India, Japan and the US are testing the waters and looking to forge a closer maritime partnership, they have also been averse to taking on China head-on. This is reflected in the exclusion of Australia from the Malabar exercises, in spite of Canberra's stated position to join the same. At the same time, these three countries have reasons to be worried about China's growing power projection capabilities in the Indian Ocean region. The scant respect China has paid to accepted international rules of conduct in its dealings with countries like Philippines have also prompted other countries in the Indo-Pacific to reassess their capabilities vis-à-vis China.

The Malabar exercises will continue to rise in importance in the near future. These exercises afforded the three nations the opportunity to test the collaboration between their personnel and the interoperability of their military platforms.

Ever since New Delhi decided not to join the Beijing-led Belt and Road Initiative (BRI), there have been some concerns that it may affect the ties. It was in May 2017 that Chinese President Xi Jinping formally launched the One Belt One Road (OBOR) initiative in Beijing. Also known as the Belt and Road Initiative (BRI), it comprises of two parts-the Silk Road Economic Belt and the 21st Century Maritime Silk Road. New Delhi did not attend the Belt and Road Initiative as it impinges on its sovereignty in the border state of Jammu and Kashmir.

Under former US President Barack Obama, the US had signalled its resolve to maintain its presence in the Asia-Pacific with the so-called "pivot" or "rebalance" to the Asia-Pacific under which it had reached out to various countries in the Asia-Pacific. It strengthened its ties with its treaty allies like Japan and the Philippines, especially as the latter has been at the receiving end of China's aggressive actions in the South China Sea region. The US has conducted repeated Freedom of Navigation Operations[6] and fly-over of territory claimed by China in the region.

India has also been at the receiving end of China's assertive actions in the region. China claims the entire Indian province of Arunachal Pradesh and has in the past refused to issue visas to high-level officials from Arunachal Pradesh. Beijing has also been issuing stapled visas to citizens from the border Indian province of Jammu and Kashmir.

India is also a net-energy importer and the continued growth of its economy depends on keeping the sea-lanes of communication in its neighbourhood open. Hence, India should keep its options open instead of jumping on to the Chinese bandwagon. Under the Modi government, India has been reaching out to countries like Vietnam and also to countries in China's backyard, like Mongolia for instance. New Delhi has always had close historical ties with countries like Indonesia too and all these ties are likely to be impacted in case China gets a stronger foothold in the Indian Ocean region. In addition, in case China were to reclaim land in the Indian Ocean region, it would be difficult for India to push it away, especially as China is a permanent veto-wielding member of the United Nations Security Council (UNSC).

The Indian Ocean is also home to tremendous natural resources, many of which are unexplored as yet. In case Beijing were to lay claims over them, it would make the case very complicated. India's trade with countries like Australia is also increasing steadily, especially as New Delhi imports a huge amount of natural resources from energy-rich Australia. All these supplies would be prone to disruption in case of an increasing Chinese foothold in the region.

If we analyse China's behaviour with regards to its territorial claims in the South China Sea, it is very clear that it is in no mood to relent on its territorial claims. Even during the visit of the Chinese President Xi Jinping to India in September 2014, Chinese troops intruded into Indian territory. Given the chain of command in China, it is highly unlikely that this would have taken place without the tacit approval of the Chinese President, Xi Jinping.

However, this is not to suggest there are only differences between India and China. India has joined the Asian Infrastructure Investment Bank (AIIB) and is also a part of the BRICS. However, economics and politics should be kept on two different tracks. While there is no harm in cooperating with Beijing on the economic front, New Delhi has to be wary on the security front as regards cooperation with Beijing.

Deng Xiaoping had said that "hide your time and bide your strength". The present Chinese leadership seems to have discarded this dictum given by Deng Xiaoping and has now adopted an openly belligerent posture. India needs to proceed with extreme caution and not be caught unawares as in 1962 when Chinese forces took India by surprise by staging a sudden attack across the Himalayas. In the light of the 2017 stand-off with China over the Doklam region of Bhutan (which is claimed by China), New Delhi would do well to heed the adage that "a stitch in time saves nine."

At the same time, the Indian Navy is also conducting a series of naval exercises with its counterparts from the ASEAN nations. In the distant past, Indian influence and culture spread to distant shores in Southeast Asia, East Asia, East Africa and many other parts of the world through the maritime realm. Even today, the island of Bali in Muslim-majority Indonesia is predominantly Hindu, attesting to the Indian influence in that part of the world. However, once India became independent in 1947, the focus turned inward and India became more of a continental power. This was partly dictated by geography and partly by necessity, as New Delhi got embroiled in land wars with its western neighbour Pakistan and a short border war with its northern neighbour, China.

However, the end of the Cold War forced India to shed its continental focus and look anew at the maritime realm. The Modi government has set its sights on increasing India's maritime footprint.

The Indian Ocean is hugely important for India's economy and its security. More than half of the world's container traffic passes through the Indian Ocean. In addition, close to 70 per cent of the total amount of the world's petroleum products pass through the waters of the Indian Ocean.[8] Besides, a large number of Indians work in the Gulf Region and send in a huge amount of remittances[9] which is very important for the health of the Indian economy.

During the visit of PM Modi to Indonesia in May last year, a new agreement was signed between India and Indonesia for the development of the Sabang port in Indonesia. As New Delhi's maritime profile increases, its connections with Southeast Asia will become even closer.

When it comes to India's physical proximity to Southeast Asia, it seldom crosses our minds that the northernmost of India's Andaman and Nicobar chain of islands lies only around 22 nautical miles from Myanmar, while the southernmost of these islands lies only around 90 nautical miles from Indonesia.

The 572 islands of India's Andaman and Nicobar archipelago are spread over an area of roughly 8,249 square kilometers and lie at the mouth of the Straits of Malacca. These straits are the second largest oil-trade choke point in the world, and it is estimated that 16 million barrels of petroleum and other liquids pass through them every day.

Recent news reports indicate that India is planning to station fighter jets in these strategically-crucial islands, which will be the first time it will do so post the Second World War. It is an indication that New Delhi realizes it needs to increase its strategic heft in these islands. Air bases in Car Nicobar and Campbell Bay on these islands could be possible bases to station fighter jets.

At present, the islands host a tri-services command,

which was set up in 2001. However, India has deployed only a helicopter unit and two Dornier aircraft permanently on these islands. In light of the importance placed on the "Act-East Policy" under the Modi government, the planned additional deployment is an important signal from New Delhi. This is especially true in the light of Prime Minister Narendra Modi's keynote address at last year's Shangri-La Dialogue in Singapore, where he laid down India's vision for the Indo-Pacific.

Indeed, India's maritime imprint in the region is growing. New Delhi conducts a host of naval exercises in the region, like the MILAN, India-Indonesia Coordinated Patrol (INDINDOCORPAT), Singapore India Maritime Bilateral Exercise (SIMBEX), and others, which involve the navies from the ASEAN countries. Besides, the Indian state-owned Oil and Natural Gas Corporation (ONGC) Videsh Limited has been scouting for oil off Vietnamese coastal waters.

So, what could be the reasons behind India's planned deployment in the Andaman and Nicobar islands ?

First, it means that New Delhi wants to add more muscle to its "Act-East Policy." While there has been a lot of emphasis on the 3C's – commerce, connectivity, and culture – in its engagement with Southeast Asia, the strategic element also needs adequate consideration. May be, New Delhi is starting to believe in "talk softly, but carry a big stick."

Second, it means that New Delhi does not want to

be caught on the wrong foot in the case of threats from both state and non-state actors. It is worth recalling here that in the case of the horrendous Mumbai terror attacks of November 2008, the attackers had come by sea. In addition, the Andaman and Nicobar Islands are also crucial in the conduct of Humanitarian Assistance and Disaster Relief (HADR) operations as seen in India's response to the devastating 2004 Indian Ocean tsunami.

Third, there are concerns in New Delhi over Beijing's growing profile in the Indian Ocean region. Earlier, in the midst of domestic turmoil in Maldives, Beijing had ticked off India when the former Maldivian President Mohamed Nasheed implored India and countries like the U.S. to intervene (though the subsequent elections have tilted the stakes back in favour of India). Similarly, in Sri Lanka, Beijing seems to have gotten the upper hand by taking over the operation of the Hambantota port on a 99-year lease.

Fourth, India did not participate in Beijing's flagship One Belt One Road (OBOR) initiative. Now New Delhi, in its own way, is trying to reach out to the ASEAN countries. Earlier in January last year, the heads of state of all the ASEAN states attended India's Republic Day celebrations in New Delhi. The planned steps by New Delhi in the Andaman and Nicobar Islands could give a sense of assurance and balance to some of the ASEAN states which have competing claims with China in the South China Sea.

India is also teaming up with Japan to develop a 15-megawatt diesel power plant in the Andaman and Nicobar

Islands. Japan has a "Free and Open Indo-Pacific Strategy," and it is worth pointing out that these islands were under Japanese control for some time during the Second World War. Japan would be the first and only foreign country which has been allowed access to these islands by India.

This could also be a part of a bigger process as India and Japan are also planning to cooperate in third countries like Sri Lanka. Japan has a base in Djibouti and hence it would be in Tokyo's interests if New Delhi bolsters its presence in the Andaman and Nicobar Islands, which also sit astride critical sea-lanes of communication. The sea lanes serve to carry oil and gas to an energy-deficient Japan, and Japanese exports pass through them on their way to key markets.

Is the maritime domain key in the developing ties between India, Japan and the ASEAN? This question has been raised by several scholars in these countries and outside and merits a deeper analysis.

First, it is worth keeping in mind that the US, India and Japan have been cooperating among themselves for quite some time now. They already have a trilateral dialogue which was first held in December 2011 and it alternates between Washington D.C., New Delhi and Tokyo. Japan is now a permanent member of the *Malabar* naval exercises, which actually started out as bilateral exercises between the United States and India.

Second, what has also brought the countries closer is the fact that India is now buying US-made military hardware, which has increased the interoperability between the armed forces of the three countries. Japan buys a huge chunk of US-made military hardware.

Third, China's growing assertiveness is one of the factors bringing these countries closer. Ever since the incident of a Chinese fishing boat ramming into Japanese court guard vessels in September 2010 near the Senkakus, relations have soured between China and Japan. The US, India, Japan and Australia were also part of an informal group, known as the Quadrilateral Initiative, which was shelved due to concerns from China. This was set up in May 2007, on the sidelines of an ASEAN Regional Forum (ARF) meeting in Manila. With India too, China has a border dispute.

China's aggressive moves in the South China Sea worry ASEAN countries like the Philippines and Vietnam. Chinese President Xi Jinping's "Maritime Silk Road" initiative has also left India in a quandary as with this move, Beijing seems to be intent on moving into what India has traditionally seen as its "own backyard". China has been trying to improve its relations with the Indian Ocean island countries like Maldives, Seychelles and Sri Lanka. It has also helped set up a series of ports in Gwadar (Pakistan), Hambantota (Sri Lanka), Chittagong (Bangladesh) and Kyaukpyu (Myanmar) in what many analysts in India describe as China's "string of pearls" strategy.

Fourth, there are economic reasons for India, Japan and the ASEAN to come closer. India is one of the fastest-growing economies in the world and both Japanese and companies from ASEAN countries stand to gain a lot from the rapidly growing Indian economy.

Fifth, the Indian Navy is the most powerful actor in the Indian Ocean region, with the sole exception of the United States. Japan is an energy-deficient country and in the light of the Fukushima disaster, Japan's nuclear energy sector has been badly hit. Hence, the Indian Navy is very critical for ensuring Japan's energy security as most of Japan's energy imports come from the Middle East. It is interesting to note that Japan and India have already started a maritime affairs dialogue.

However, it is worth remembering that, unlike Japan, which is a treaty ally of the US, it is very unlikely that India will be drawn into a formal alliance with the US. There are still some vocal sections in India, which are against any kind of rapprochement with the US. The problem is also compounded by the fact that though Osama bin Laden was found and killed in a raid in Pakistan, American support to Pakistan continues. At the same time, it is also very apparent that while non-alignment was the mantra for earlier Indian governments, for the Modi government, the new mantra seems to be, multi-alignment.

There are also many opportunities for cooperation between Japan, India and the ASEAN countries in multilateral forums like the East Asia Summit and the G20. All said and done, the growing convergence between India, Japan and the ASEAN is a reflection of the times. As the increasing use of the term, Indo-Pacific, reflects, shared security and economic concerns will ensure that India, Japan and the ASEAN grow ever closer in the years to come.

NEW DELHI'S INDO-PACIFIC STRATEGY

New Delhi has a benign presence in the region and, hence, any Indian deployment (in the Andaman and Nicobar Islands) should not worry its neighbours in the region. As the maritime focus in India's "Act-East Policy" increases, these kinds of deployments will give New Delhi more options on the table when it comes to its presence and influence in the wider Indian Ocean region.

Prime Minister Modi in his Shangri-La Dialogue address last year clearly outlined that India's engagement with the world would be based on "peace, respect, dialogue and absolute commitment to international law."[10] As the term Indo-Pacific gains increasing currency, New Delhi's decision to deploy fighter jets in the Andaman and Nicobar Islands comes not a day to soon.

In his seminal book, *The Influence of Sea Power Upon History 1660-1783,* the renowned naval historian, Alfred Thayer Mahan, noted that it was the British Navy which stood between Napolean and his domination of the world. Similarly, as New Delhi aspires to play a bigger role on the global stage by pitching for permanent membership of the United Nations Security Council (UNSC), its Navy will remain an important force multiplier.

As outlined above, the Indian Navy plays a key role in ensuring the safety and security of the country's sea-lanes of communication. This is important since India is a net-energy importer. In addition, the Navy has played a key role in the evacuation of Indian nationals from various conflict zones as could be seen in Yemen. It has been taking part in the *Milan* series of naval exercises along with the navies of various nations from Southeast Asia and beyond. India's Navy is keen to increase its interoperability with the navies of many countries. This kind of interoperability is not only restricted to the security domain, but also extends to areas like anti-piracy efforts and disaster relief. India had joined hands with countries like the US, Australia, Japan and Indonesia to provide rescue and recovery efforts in the wake of the Boxing Day tsunami of 2004 while at the same time, the Indian Navy has also been very proactive in anti-piracy efforts in the Indian Ocean region.

All said and done, the Indian Navy will play an increasingly proactive role in the coming years and months in the Indo-Pacific waters. India's Indian Maritime Security Strategy (IMSS-2015) also "acknowledges the hybrid nature of maritime challenges – the blurring of lines between traditional and non-traditional threats"[12]. As in the past, who commands the waves will be one of the key determinants of who calls the shots on the high table of international geopolitics.

MAJOR CHALLENGES FOR INDIA IN THE MARITIME ARENA

However, India faces significant challenges in the maritime domain. Its submarine fleet has suffered a string of mishaps in the last couple of years. As far as the Indian

Navy's share of the defence budget is concerned, it stood at a dismal 16 per cent of the total defence budget for 2015-16, while the Army got 53 per cent.[13] New Delhi would also have to step up the indigenisation process of its defence hardware, especially of its Navy.

Non-traditional security threats like terrorism, piracy, people-trafficking etc. also present significant challenges for India in the maritime arena. New Delhi has borne the brunt of terrorist attacks through the sea as seen in the horrendous Mumbai 2008 attacks. However, coastal security still remains a concern especially as India has a huge coastline of around 7516.6 km.[14]

WHAT IS CHINA'S INDIAN OCEAN STRATEGY?

China's Maritime Silk Road (MSR) initiative is part of its overall "One Belt One Road" (OBOR) initiative that has been initiated by President Xi Jinping, who has often talked about the so-called *Chinese Dream*. The OBOR is in many ways a re-invention of the ancient Chinese Silk Roads which ran from China to Europe and branched off to various countries including India. The other part of the "One Belt One Road" is the "Silk Road Economic Belt,"[15] through which China is trying to build land connectivity through the Central Asian countries to Europe.

China is a net energy importer and one of the fastest growing economies in the world. Its gargantuan appetite for energy has seen it import energy resources from various parts of the world. Beijing has slowly, but steadily been trying to assert its presence in the Indian Ocean and beyond. It declared a new Air Defence Identification Zone (ADIZ) over the East China Sea in 2013, which was promptly rejected by Japan, US and countries like South Korea. It has also been involved in a tense standoff with the Philippines and has proceeded with the installation of missile batteries in the Woody Island in the Paracel group of islands in the South China Sea.

Various observers have doubted China's real intentions in the South China Sea region. They are fearful that China may go ahead and declare an Air Defence Identification Zone in the region. The former commander of the US Pacific Fleet Admiral Harry B Harris has cautioned that China was building "a great wall of sand"[16] in the South China Sea. At a speech at the Raisina Dialogue in India in March 2016, he noted that "expanded cooperation with India will not only be the defining partnership for the Rebalance, it will arguably be the defining partnership for America in the 21st century."[17]

Meanwhile, it is worthwhile to remember that in the past, Australia, India, Japan and the US had come together for the Quadrilateral Initiative, which however, had to be rescinded in the light of protestations from Beijing.

In addition, China has been trying to woo the new government in Myanmar especially after the exit of the military junta in Myanmar made Beijing jittery as to its long-term interests in the country. In addition, for the first time, China has set up a military base in Djibouti which will help China establish a foothold in a very strategic location.

INDIAN AND CHINESE INTERESTS IN THE INDIAN OCEAN REGION

India has always been the resident power in the Indian Ocean region with the sole exception of the United States. Its Navy has had a commanding presence in the region between the Strait of Hormuz and the Strait of Malacca while its Andaman and Nicobar chain of islands lie at the entrance of the Strait of Malacca, which has been termed by many observers as China's "Achilles Heel". The setting up of a tri-services command by India in the Andaman and Nicobar islands, gives it an unmatched reach in the region.

Zhang Ming, an influential Chinese naval analyst has flagged that "the 244 islands which are a part of India's Andaman and Nicobar chain of islands could be used as a "metal chain" to block the western entrance to the Strait of Malacca"[18]. Though this is not an official position of Beijing, it means that surely there are people in China who think in that manner. However, in the hoary past too, China had tried to carve out its influence in the maritime arena in India's neighbourhood with people like Admiral Zheng. He spreading Chinese influence far and wide. Aeons ago, the state (province) of Kerala in India's southern coast grew accustomed to Chinese fishing nets.[19]

Second, in many cases, India's interests in the neighbourhood are at odds with those of Beijing. For example, New Delhi has always had close ties with the island nations in the region like Sri Lanka, Maldives and Seychelles. However, of late, once again, Beijing has been rapidly trying to make inroads into what New Delhi has traditionally seen as its own "backyard".

Third, a clear pattern emerges from China's diplomatic forays into India's maritime neighbourhood. During the visit of Chinese President Xi Jinping to Sri Lanka in 2014, an MoU was signed for the Colombo Port city project, but was suspended later following the election of a new President, Maithripala Sirisena, who took over from the previous President, Mahinda Rajapaksa, who was seen as being more close to China. However, the stalled project has now been revived. Earlier, Chinese submarines had also made calls at Sri Lankan ports, much to the chagrin of New Delhi.

Sri Lanka's importance for India also lies in the fact that there is a sizeable minority of Tamils of Indian origin in Sri Lanka and India had sent the Indian Peace Keeping Force (IPKF) to Sri Lanka to take on the feared Liberation Tigers of Tamil Ealam (LTTE) in 1987. Another country in India's neighbourhood, Maldives, had cancelled the contract given to an Indian infrastructure major GMR for the expansion of the international airport in its capital, Male. The contract was later given to a Chinese firm, which clearly shows Beijing's growing influence in the region.

During the visit of Chinese President Xi Jinping to Pakistan in April 2015, an announcement was made for a China-Pakistan Economic Corridor (CPEC)[20] which will run from Kashgar in Western China to Gwadar in Pakistan on the Arabian Sea front, allowing Beijing to bypass the

Strait of Malacca and avoid what has been euphemistically dubbed as the "Malacca Dilemma". In addition, it has also repeatedly blocked India's bid for membership of the Nuclear Suppliers' Group (NSG).

Fourth, India was also taken aback when China put a technical hold on its attempts to have Pakistan-based terror outfit Jaish-e-Mohammad's chief Maulana Mohammed Azhar designated as a terrorist at the United Nations. This clearly shows that China has double standards when it comes to dealing with terrorists. While it considers Uyghur separatists as terrorists, they have applied a different standard when it comes to Pakistan-based terrorists. Even after the horrendous Pulwama terror attack in India in February 2019, which killed more than 40 para military troopers, China has refused to budge from its stand.

India has always aspired for a benign security environment in its neighbourhood, which will help it to take care of its own needs of domestic development. However, it has been at the receiving end of terrorism emanating from Pakistan as evidenced by incidents like the attack on the Indian Parliament (December 2001), the Mumbai terror attacks of November 2008, the Pathankot terror attack of January 2016 and the Pulwama terror attack of February 2019. Hence China's "all-weather friendship" with Pakistan is worrisome for India, especially given the fact that Beijing has been alleged to supply nuclear and missile know-how to Pakistan.

India needs to give up on *ad hoc* measures with regards

to its foreign policy and needs to think on a bigger scale. Former Indian PM, Dr Manmohan Singh had termed that "Asia is big enough for both India and China to grow". However, in spite of the visit of PM Modi to China in April 2018 for the Wuhan Summit, things have not improved drastically between the two neighbours.President Xi Jinping is taking a hard-line position on the foreign policy front to shore up his domestic credentials.

NOTES

1. Indian Navy, Indian Naval Doctrine 2015, available at https://www.indiannavy.nic.in/content/indian-maritimedoctrine-2015-version accessed on February 17, 2019.
2. United States Navy, U.S., Indian and Japanese Maritime Forces to Participate in Exercise Malabar 2018, https://www.navy.mil/submit/display.asp?story_id=105908 accessed on February 22, 2019.
3. Ministry of External Affairs, Prime Minister's Keynote Address at Shangri La Dialogue (June 01, 2018), available at https://www.mea.gov.in/Speeches-Statements.htm?dtl29943/Prime+Ministers+Keynote+Address+at+Shangri+La+Dialogue+June+01+2018 accessed on February 22, 2019.
4. Outlook India, Maritime Security Key Dimension of Bilateral Ties: Swaraj, https://www.outlookindia.com/newswire/story/maritime-security-key-dimension-ofbilateral-ties-swaraj/886967 accessed on February 22, 2019.
5. Department of Defense, Remarks by Secretary Mattis at Plenary Session of the 2018 Shangri-La Dialogue, available

at https://dod.defense.gov/News/Transcripts/Transcript-View/Article/1538599/remarks-by-secretary-mattis-atplenary-session-of-the-2018-shangri-la-dialogue/ accessed on January 21, 2019.

6. Idress Ali, U.S. to boost South China Sea freedom of navigation moves, Admiral says available at http://www.reuters.com/article/ussouthchinasea-usa-idUSKCN0VX22B accessed on September 17, 2018.
7. *The Hindu*, Mr. Modi's Ocean View available at http://www.thehindu.com/opinion/editorial/mr-modis-oceanview/article7000182.ece accessed on October 10 , 2019.
8. Robert Kaplan, Power Plays in the Indian Ocean available at file:///C:/Users/Acer/Downloadsch_6_CNAS+Contested+Commons_0-11%20(2).pdf accessed on October 10, 2018.
9. NDTV Profit, India Largest Remittances Receiving Country in 2015: World Bank available at http://profit.ndtv.com/news/economy/article-india-largestremittances-receiving-country-in-2015-worldbank-1256720 accessed on August 10, 2018.
10. Ministry of External Affairs, Prime Minister 's Keynote Address at Shangri La Dialogue (June 01, 2018), available at https://www.mea.gov.in/Speeches-Statements.htm?dtl/29943/Prime+Ministers+Keynote+Address+at+Shangri+La+Dialogue+June+01+2018.
11. Press Information Bureau(2013), First Japan-India Maritime Exercise (JIMEX) in Indian Waters From 19-22 Dec available at http://pib.nic.in/newsite/Print Release.aspx?relid=101825 accessed on August 25, 2018.

12. Abhijit Singh, India's New Maritime Security Strategy: 'Brand-building' in an Era of 'Geopolitical Discord' available at http://www.idsa.in/idsacomments/indias-new-maritime-security-strategy_asingh_211215 accessed on September 7, 2018.
13. Laxman K Behera, India's Defence Budget 2015-16, available at http://www.idsa.in/issuebrief/Indias DefenceBudget 2015-16_lkbehera_020315 accessed on October 5, 2018.
14. Database on coastal states of India available at http://io menvis.nic.in/index2.aspx?slid=758&sublinkid=119&langid=1&mid=1 accessed on October 1, 2019.
15. Xinhua, Chronology of China's Belt and Road Initiative, available at http://news.xinhuanet.com/english/ 2015-03/28/c_134105435.htm accessed on September 21, 2018.
16. Voice of America(2015), US Admiral: China 'Creating a Great Wall of Sand' in Sea, available at http://www.voanews.com/content/us-adminral-china-creating-agreat-wall-of-sand-in-sea/2700920.html accessed on September 7, 2019.
17. Admiral Harry B Harris, Raisina Dialogue Remarks- "Let's Be Ambitious Together" available at http://www.pacom.mil/Media/SpeechesTestimony/tabid/6706/Article/683842/raisina-dialogue-remarks-lets-beambitious-together.aspx accessed on September 29, 2018.
18. Borah, Rupakjyoti, The Maritime Silk Road in China's OBOR. How Should India respond, Aziya Sekkai, Journal of the Japan Association for Asian Studies, Vol. 64 No 3, July 2018.
19. Shashi Tharoor, Pax Indica, India and the World of the 21st century, Allen Lane, New Delhi.

20. BBC News, "China's Xi Jinping agrees $46bnsuper; highway to Pakistan", available at http://www.bbc.com/news/world-asia-32377088 accessed on October 2 , 2018.

5

THE US AND CHINA FACTORS

THE US FACTOR

The election of President Trump in the US has given rise to a new era in Washington's ties with countries across the world and many of these countries are trying to figure out how to deal with the Trump Administration and the maverick President himself. At the same time, the growing bonhomie between India and the US has been one of the defining features of New Delhi's foreign policy in the period after the end of the Cold War. During this period, India embarked on what is now known as the "Act-East Policy" (earlier known as the "Look-East Policy"), besides opening up its economy. This marked a sea-change in India's foreign policy after its independence, since it had inched closer to the erstwhile Soviet Union, until its dissolution.

Although Indo-US relations went into a tailspin following New Delhi's nuclear tests of 1998, things rebounded quickly with the visit of the then US President Bill Clinton to India in March 2000. The next major step in the bilateral ties was the signing of the Indo-US civilian nuclear deal in October 2008, which led to the end of India's pariah status when it came to nuclear trade.

Former Indian PM Manmohan Singh was the first state guest of the Obama Administration in November 2009 and though relations once again went into a freefall towards the end of the second term of the Obama Administration, they were back on track after PM Modi took over in India in May 2014. He paid a visit to the US in late September that year and soon thereafter, former US President Barack Obama was the Chief Guest at India's Republic Day celebrations in January 2015.

After President Trump took office in January 2017, New Delhi and Washington have come even closer. A host of factors are bringing India and the US closer in a way like never before and they merit a deeper analysis.

ECONOMIC FACTORS

The Indian economy is one of the fastest growing economies in the world and is a market which no American company can ignore. An array of American companies are present in the Indian market and they are doing well. The Indian aviation market is one of the biggest across the world and companies like Boeing are doing brisk business in India. Meanwhile, Indian I-T firms are also doing good business in the US and employ many Americans too.

Former US Secretary of State, Rex Tillerson, noted in a major policy speech in October 2017 "as our economies grow closer, we find more opportunities for prosperity for our people. More than 600 American companies operate in India. U.S. foreign direct investment has jumped by 500 percent in the past two years alone. And last year, our bilateral trade hit a record of roughly $115 billion, a number we plan to increase." At the same time, Indian companies like Tata Consultancy Services (TCS), Wipro, Essar America, Piramal, Mahindra etc. are doing well in the US market.

STRATEGIC FACTORS

After the Modi government was sworn in, India has gone ahead to sign the Logistics Exchange Memorandum of Understanding (LEMOA) with the US–which allows Indian and American forces access to designated military facilities for refuelling and replenishment. This is a big leap forward for India as New Delhi had earlier been wary of signing any such deal with the US and marks a decisive break in Indian foreign policy from its earlier ideological moorings. One of the major tenets of Indian foreign policy in the period after its independence had been nonalignment, but now it seems that it has been given the go-bye in favour of multi-alignment.

Both India and the US also share concerns about China's growing aggressiveness in the Indo-Pacific region. The joint statement released during the visit of former US President Barack Obama to India in January 2015 notes that "we affirm the importance of safeguarding maritime security and ensuring freedom of navigation and over flight throughout the region, especially in the South China Sea."

This was a first for India, as New Delhi had avoided making explicit mention of the South China Sea dispute. In addition, New Delhi is wary of Beijing's attempts to make greater forays into the Indian Ocean region with its so-called "String of Pearls" strategy. Under this policy, Beijing has helped with the construction of ports in Bangladesh, Pakistan, Sri Lanka. China also now has its first overseas base in Djibouti.

New Delhi has not joined the Beijing-led "Belt and Road Initiative" because of concerns over the violation of its sovereignty. The US too has stayed away from the BRI (also known as the OBOR), though it did send a representative to the BRI meeting in Beijing in May 2017. Hence, there could be possibilities for cooperation between the US and India in the field of infrastructure too. Meanwhile, in 2017, India and China narrowly avoided a major skirmish in the Doklam region of Bhutan, where Chinese troops had started constructing a road (in what they consider as their own territory). The standoff was resolved after almost two months.

In addition, new opportunities for cooperation are also emerging in the field of energy as the US has begun to export energy to India and New Delhi is a net-energy importer. Energy security is now an important determinant of India's foreign policy and this is where cooperation with American firms could be key. New Delhi and Washington are also cooperating in the field of nuclear energy and US-based Westinghouse will be setting up nuclear reactors in India as part of the Indo-US civilian nuclear deal.

At the same time, India has emerged as a big market for American defence manufacturers. This is a far cry from the times when India almost solely depended on Russia for its supply of military hardware. New Delhi is one of the biggest arms importers in the world. It was in 2005 that a "New Framework for India-US Defense Relations" was signed. The US has now recognized India as a "major defence partner" and New Delhi has now bought military hardware worth over US$13 billion from the US. The recognition of India as a major defence partner in June 2016 allows for the transfer of technology to India, which is also a major plank of PM Narendra Modi's "Make in India" campaign pledge.

COMMON INTERESTS IN THE INDO-PACIFIC

Under the Obama administration, the US had launched the so-called "pivot" to the Asia-Pacific. While President Trump has not dumped the so-called "pivot", he and members of his administration have been increasingly using the term "Indo-Pacific", which clearly reflects the increasing importance accorded to India by the Trump Administration.

During his speech at the APEC CEO Summit at Da Nang in Vietnam in November 2017, President Trump remarked that "I've had the honor of sharing our vision for a free and open Indo-Pacific – a place where sovereign and independent nations, with diverse cultures and many different dreams, can all prosper side-by-side, and thrive in freedom and in peace."[1]

In November 2017, President Trump completed an Asian tour, which took him to Japan, South Korea, China, Vietnam and the Philippines, thereby, in many ways, setting at rest questions regarding the US distancing itself from Asia, especially in the light of its withdrawal from the Trans-Pacific Partnership (TPP). PM Modi met President Trump for a bilateral summit in June 2017 besides interacting with him on the sidelines of many multilateral meetings. On the sidelines of the East Asia Summit (EAS) in Manila in November 2017, the two leaders "pledged to enhance their cooperation as major defense partners, resolving that two of the world's great democracies should also have the world's greatest militaries."[2]

OTHER FACTORS

At the people-to-people level too, Indians have risen to the highest ranks in some of the top US corporations and also in American bureaucracy. The 3.5 million-plus strong Indian Diaspora in the US has also helped to bring the two countries closer.

In addition, the burgeoning relations between India and the US have also been helped by the growing bonhomie between India and US allies like Japan and Australia. Japanese PM Shinzo Abe has built a close rapport with President Trump and also has a very good equation with Indian PM Modi as well.

The de-hyphenation of US-India and US-Pakistan ties has also helped to bring India and the US closer. This has become more pronounced after Osama bin Laden was traced to Abbottabad in Pakistan.

AREAS OF CONCERN IN INDIA-US TIES

However, it is not as if all is well between the two sides. The issue of H1 visas is a major stumbling block as President Donald Trump (many a times in the past) has talked about slashing numbers for H1 visas and Indians are one of the biggest beneficiaries of the H1 visas.

The two countries also do not see eye to eye on some issues like Syria and also since India maintains close ties with Russia, especially on the defence front.

There could also be issues with New Delhi's relations with countries like Iran. New Delhi has recently opened a new trade route with Afghanistan (and Central Asia) via the port of Chabahar in Iran. However, after the coming of the Trump Administration to power, US' relations with Iran have once again been pushed to the backburner and this might impact India's fledgling ties with Iran.

There are also issues regarding Washington's relations with Pakistan. New Delhi has had problems with Islamabad because of its backing of anti-India terror groups operating out of Pakistan and would like to see Washington use its leverage over Islamabad to rein in such terror groups.

In addition, Trump's penchant for cutting deals with the likes of China may also damage the relations with India, since New Delhi would be loath to accept a China-dominated Asia.

THE ROAD AHEAD IN INDIA-US TIES

India under the Modi administration has also been getting close to Israel. PM Modi became the first-ever Indian PM to visit Israel. Given President Trump's views on Israel and keeping his domestic audience in mind, India, Israel and Washington are also likely to get closer under Trump and Modi.

India wants to get into key international forums like the Nuclear Suppliers' Group (NSG) and has been pitching for full membership of the United Nations Security Council (UNSC) for which it has already secured the backing of the US. During PM Modi's visit to the US in June 2017, President Trump "reaffirmed the support of the United States for India's permanent membership on a reformed U.N. Security Council."[3]

Although there are still many issues of divergence between India and the US, the possible areas of cooperation far outweigh the areas of divergence. Hence, the two countries should look at the bigger picture and should not be in a situation where they can't see the wood for the trees. As PM Modi noted in his speech to the US Congress in June 2016, there seems to be a "new symphony in play" in the Indo-US bilateral relationship.

WHAT HAS BROUGHT INDIA AND US CLOSER?

First, the US and India have common concerns regarding terrorism emanating from countries like Pakistan. During the 2008 Mumbai terrorist attacks in India, many American nationals also lost their lives. They also have a common interests in the stability of Afghanistan. Although, India has not committed troops to Afghanistan, it is one of the biggest donors in Afghanistan and has been involved in reconstruction work all across Afghanistan.

Second, India is an important part of the US' "Indo-Pacific" strategy. As China's power rises in the Indo-Pacific, the US is looking for more and more countries to help it keep its pre-eminent position intact in the region. Third, the US has now emerged as one of the biggest defence suppliers to India, in sharp contrast to the days of the Cold War.

It is ironical that the world's oldest and biggest democracies, the United States and India, respectively, stayed aloof for much of the Cold War era. Similar was the case of relations between Japan and India, Asia's two oldest democracies. During the Cold War era, India, though it proclaimed itself to be a non-aligned nation, had actually inched closer to the erstwhile Soviet Union, especially after the signing of the Indo-Soviet Treaty of Friendship and Cooperation in 1971. The end of the Cold War and the dissolution of the erstwhile Soviet Union left India with no options, but to move closer to countries like the United States and Japan. It was also during this period that India began to liberalise its economy and launched what was then known as the "Look-East Policy" (which has now been renamed as the "Act East Policy"), which meant reinvigorating India's historical ties with the countries of Southeast Asia and East Asia.

THE CHINA FACTOR

In April 2017, the Dalai Lama concluded his 9-day visit to India's border state of Arunachal Pradesh, amidst much brouhaha, both inside and outside the country. While the Dalai Lama had visited Tawang before (his last visit was in 2009), this visit in 2017 was very significant as Beijing, in the run-up to the visit, raised a howl of protest that the Dalai Lama should not be allowed to go to the mountain town. China claims Tawang to be a part of what it calls "Southern Tibet." Tawang is also the birthplace of the sixth Dalai Lama.

Beijing also took umbrage at the fact that India's Minister of State for Home, Kiren Rijiju (himself a Member of Parliament from Arunachal Pradesh), accompanied the Dalai Lama during some sections of the trip. Incidentally, before heading to Arunachal Pradesh, the Dalai Lama also took part in the "Namami Brahmaputra" festival in Guwahati in the Indian province of Assam. It was also attended by India's former President Pranab Mukherjee. Incidentally, the Brahmaputra river starts its journey as the *Yarlung Tsangpo* river in Tibet, China.

RAMIFICATIONS OF THE VISIT

There were several important ramifications of this visit of the Dalai Lama.

First, it meant that New Delhi, as on many past occasions, will not be cowed down by pressure emanating from Beijing. PM Modi commands a huge majority in

India, and has a keen rapport with many world leaders – something which Beijing needs to keep in mind.

Second, it means that New Delhi may not be averse to allowing the Dalai Lama to Arunachal Pradesh, although it has made it clear that it accepts Tibet as an integral part of China and has accepted the "One-China Policy."

In response to China's criticism, Kiren Rijiju said, "When India has never interfered in Beijing's affairs, and has respected the 'One China' policy, China should not interfere in India's internal affairs or object to the Dalai Lama's visit."[4]

Third, China will have to rethink how it acts in its neighbourhood. It is worth noting that China is already embroiled in territorial disputes with India, Vietnam, the Philippines, and Japan. Fourth, India will have to stand guard since Beijing may retaliate on other fronts. In the field of trade, India already runs a huge trade deficit with China. Beijing has also been smarting under the onslaught of US President Donald Trump's latest moves in Syria and North Korea.

On one hand, US President Donald Trump authorized missile strikes on Syria even as he was having summit level talks with the Chinese President Xi Jinping. On the North Korean issue, Trump has threatened to go it alone, in case China does not cooperate with the US. Hence, China may try to send a message to the world, by hitting out at India and Indian interests.

FUTURE OF SINO-INDIAN TIES

Although Beijing was quick to make known its displeasure with India over the Dalai Lama issue, it has been acting with disdain toward India's wishes and interests. China has repeatedly blocked India's bid for membership in the Nuclear Suppliers' Group (NSG). Beijing has also scuttled New Delhi's attempts at putting Pakistan-based terrorist Maulana Masood Azhar on a United Nations watchlist. It has not come out either in support of India's bid to become a permanent member of the UN Security Council. In addition, in spite of New Delhi's protestations, Beijing has been pumping money into the China-Pakistan Economic Corridor (CPEC), which runs through parts of Pakistan-occupied Kashmir (PoK).

The new normal in Sino-Indian ties could be that while there would be cooperation on the economic front, the political ties could be in for a period of upheaval. Various articles in the Chinese media had hit out at India for "allowing" the Dalai Lama visit to Tawang. The *Global Times* noted that "with a GDP several times higher than that of India, military capabilities that can reach the Indian Ocean and having good relations with India's peripheral nations, coupled with the fact that India's turbulent northern state borders China, if China engages in a geopolitical game with India, will Beijing lose to New Delhi?"[5]

The other issue that could negatively impact Sino-Indian ties is the question of a successor to the Dalai Lama. What if the Dalai Lama anoints his successor from someone in India? This is bound to be a bone of contention between China and India in the near future.

By standing firm on its stance to allow the Dalai Lama to go ahead with his visit to Tawang in 2017, New Delhi has clearly laid down new rules of engagement with Beijing. China would do well to factor in this new reality when dealing with India on future issues of bilateral and multilateral concern. At the same time, India should not let its guard down even though the Dalai Lama's Tawang visit had passed off peacefully, lest it be caught on the wrong foot as in 1962.

THE WUHAN SUMMIT AND AFTER

An informal summit between Indian PM Narendra Modi and Chinese President Xi Jinping at Wuhan in China on April 27-28 last year took many by surprise, not only in India and China, but in many other parts of the world. This was indeed a welcome augury after the sabre-rattling between the two countries in 2017 when China started constructing a road in the Doklam region of Bhutan (claimed by China) and India intervened on the side of Bhutan.

As it was an informal summit, there were no "takeaways" as such from the meeting, but it did reflect an easing of tensions between the two Asian behemoths.

WHY CHINA MAY HAVE AGREED TO WUHAN?

Beijing had its own reasons for the meeting.

First, the rapid pace of events on the Korean peninsula

meant that Beijing has lost its traditional role in the region and there is no guarantee that the US would pull out its forces from South Korea–which means that it could be a double whammy for Beijing.

Second, China is also in the midst of a trade war with the US with President Trump breathing down hard on China. Beijing runs a huge trade surplus with New Delhi and therefore has a lot to gain from improved ties with India.

Third, this is part of Beijing's attempts to reach out to countries like Japan and India-countries which can afford not to toe Beijing's line. As opposed to that, reports which indicate that China has installed anti-ship cruise missiles and surface-to-air missiles in the Spratly islands in the South China Sea mean that it has not had a real change of heart.

The Wuhan Summit therefore afforded both the parties an opportunity to gauge each other. While it is good news that both the sides are back on the negotiating table, New Delhi should avoid lowering its guard and understand that the temporary olive branch by Beijing to India, could be part of a bigger game-plan. As they say, one swallow does not make a summer.

After much brouhaha, it was indeed welcome augury when both China and India decided to withdraw their respective forces from the Doklam area of Bhutan. The two Asian behemoths had been locked in a stalemate since June 16, 2017, when China started constructing a road through Bhutanese territory.

What surprised most observers, especially in India, was the swiftness of China's volte-face on Doklam, although its state-owned media had gone hammer and tongs at New Delhi and the Indian government ever since the crisis broke out.

On August 28, 2017, the Indian Ministry of External Affairs in a statement noted that "expeditious disengagement of border personnel at the face-off site at Doklam has been agreed to and is ongoing." On the same day, the Chinese Foreign Ministry spokesperson remarked that "the Indian side withdrew all its border personnel and equipment that were illegally on the Chinese territory to the Indian side. The Chinese personnel onsite have verified this situation. China will continue fulfilling its sovereign rights to safeguard territorial sovereignty in compliance with the stipulations of the border-related historical treaty."

WHAT TO EXPECT NOW

This year, 2019, is an election year in India and PM Modi knows all too well that the economy will need a booster shot in order to improve his chances of re-election. The "Make-In-India" programme has not had the kind of success that was originally planned for. Hence, injection of Chinese capital in areas like infrastructure will be good for the health of the Indian economy. New Delhi would also like to cushion some of the impact of China's already close ties with Pakistan. There are also reports that China and India may not be averse to cooperating in Afghanistan.

There are still lot of problems between the two sides. India has opted to stay out of the Belt and Road Initiative (BRI) or the OBOR and is unlikely to change its stand on the same, especially as it involves sovereignty concerns. On the other hand, China is unlikely to give up its claims on the Indian state of Arunachal Pradesh or stop its dalliance with Pakistan.

China has also been rapidly moving into India's neighbourhood, whether it be in Sri Lanka, Pakistan or the Maldives and New Delhi has not been able to come up with a coherent strategy on how to respond to this. Though India had signed on to the Quad along with the US, Japan and Australia, it seems to be caught in a bind (along with Japan) on how to take it forward.

China is already hurting under the impact of India's boycott of the One Belt One Road or the Belt and Road forum in Beijing in May 2017. After Doklam, Beijing would surely be nursing a big grievance. Hence, it will be no surprise if it repeatedly stymies India's efforts on the international stage, like New Delhi's bid to become a permanent member of the United Nations Security Council and the Nuclear Suppliers' Group (NSG).

New Delhi could also see a stronger Chinese tilt towards Pakistan and more belligerence from Beijing in the Indian Ocean region. New Delhi is reaching out to Southeast Asia and East Asia through its "Act-East Policy," and Beijing would make even greater efforts to scuttle India's forays into these regions.

China is unlikely to be happy with New Delhi

"intransigence" on the Doklam issue, which has halted the Chinese juggernaut after the easy "victories" it has achieved over countries like the Philippines as far as territorial claims are concerned. That said, while Beijing may not immediately come back to Doklam, there are chances that the PLA may intrude at other areas, where the Indian armed forces are at a weaker position than at Doklam.

China did not share hydrological data with India in 2017 as per earlier agreements with lower riparian countries like India for rivers flowing through and originating in its Tibet region. In 2017, India, Nepal, and Bangladesh suffered severe flooding, and Beijing was not very keen to do its part by sharing the hydrological data, especially with India.

Tokyo will also have to be careful as China might increase the heat on Japan so as to divert public opinion in the light of its climb-down on Doklam, maybe by sending more fishing vessels to the Senkakus. Since Tokyo needs Beijing's help on North Korea, it would have limited options when dealing with such aggressiveness from Beijing and needs to be prepared in advance. After the end of the Doklam standoff, the usually strident *Global Times* has also adopted a conciliatory tone, and in an article remarked that "China needs to enhance its deterrence to avoid external provocations. China has powerful comprehensive strength, while how we utilize this strength to safeguard our national interests hasn't been recognized by external forces and has to be proved in a crisis."

In Doklam, China was caught on a sticky wicket, but

the next time round, it may well choose the timing and place of its move, in order to catch India on the backfoot. The sudden volte-face from Beijing on Doklam is too good to be true, and if New Delhi takes this Chinese stance at face value, it would only be at its own peril.

NOTES

1. The White House, Remarks by President Trump at APECCEO Summit | Da Nang, Vietnam, available at https://www.whitehouse.gov/briefings-statements/remarkspresident-trump-apec-ceo-summit-da-nang-vietnam/ accessed on February 26, 2019.
2. Hindustan Times, India and US should have 'world's greatest militaries', say Modi and Trump, available at https://www.hindustantimes.com/world-news/india-andusshould-have-world-s-greatest-militaries-say-modi-andtrump/story-LldRrtB7sJpioZzZyNqG0M.html accessed on February 26, 2019.
3. Times of India, Trump supports India's permanent membership of UNSC available at http://timesofindia.indiatimes.com/articleshow/59335826.cms? utm_source=contentofinterest&utm_medium=text& utm_campaign=cppst accessed on February 26, 2019.
4. The Hindu, As Dalai Lama visits Arunachal Pradesh, China vows to take 'necessary measures', https://www.thehindu.com/news/national/china-vows-necessarymeasure-after-dalai-lama-visits-arunachal-pradesh/article17824312.ece accessed on January 26, 2019.
5. Global Times, India's use of Dalai Lama card tactless, http://www.globaltimes.cn/content/1041035.shtml accessed on February 26, 2019.

6

A 20-POINT AGENDA FOR 2020

The Northeastern states of India have immense potential, but there are quite a few challenges, too, which they face. These include:

1. Lack of Industrial Base and Employment Opportunities

The states (provinces) in Northeast India suffer from a lack of industrialization. Employment opportunities are few and far between, while levels of literacy are relatively higher than some other parts of the country. This has created a problem of hordes of educated unemployed youths, some of whom have taken to militancy.

2. Natural Disasters

Then, there are natural disasters that these parts of the country regularly face. For example, the Northeastern states regularly suffer from floods, landslides, mudslides etc. thereby bringing immense misery to the people of the region and destroying the infrastructure.

3. Lack of Good-Quality Infrastructure

With regards to the development of infrastructure in the region, there are still significant challenges-both in terms of injection of funding and technological expertise.

4. Lack of Adequate Co-ordination Between State Governments

There is also lack of adequate coordination between the different state governments of Northeast India, which adds to the problems faced by the region.

5. Lack of Air Connectivity

Northeastern states are plagued by lack of air connectivity with the ASEAN countries. For example, if one were to fly from say Guwahati to Hanoi in Vietnam, he or she would need to change aircrafts either in Kolkata, Delhi or in Chennai and then travel to Hanoi. At present, even to travel to say Yangon from NE India, they would need to travel in the opposite direction before heading to Yangon.

POLICY RECOMMENDATIONS

1. Increasing the Co-ordination Between State Governments in the Region

This is a major factor, which will be *sine qua non* to improving the development levels in the Northeast. At the moment, there is inadequate coordination between the state governments of the region. It has also been the case that in the past, different states of the Northeast have had different political parties in power and that has not helped matters. The coordination between the different state governments of Northeast Indian states and those of the ASEAN countries also needs to be increased.

2. Increasing the Air Connectivity Between India and the ASEAN and Beyond to Japan

The development of air connectivity between India

and the ASEAN will be key to the next-level of the ties between the two. There are plenty of airports, which can be connected to the ASEAN. For example, Guwahati can be well connected with ASEAN. Then there are the smaller airports in the region, besides helipads. In order to improve the air connectivity, low-cost-carriers from both India as well as the ASEAN countries could also play a major role.

3. Increasing Tourist Arrivals in NE India from the ASEAN Countries

It will also be important to increase tourist arrivals from the ASEAN countries to NE India given the complementarities between the two regions in terms of culture, food etc. There should be a special thrust on the Buddhist element in the ties. The Northeastern states of India should be promoted as a whole to tourists from the ASEAN countries and also from Japan. There is huge potential especially for inbound tourism from the ASEAN countries to NE India. For example, there are still some communities known as the Tai-Phakes who reside in Upper Assam and follow the same way of life as followed by their ancestors in Southeast Asia. Several dignitaries especially from Thailand have visited the Tai-Phake village. In addition, Mawlynnong village in the Northeastern state of Meghalaya has been named by BBC Travel as Asia's cleanest village.[1] Then there is the Kaziranga National Park, which is home to the famed one-horned rhinoceros. Nowadays there are various festivals which are held in Northeast India like the Hornbill Festival in Nagaland and many others which could be a big draw for tourists from the ASEAN countries. Northeast India is home to some of the most scenic and exotic locales in India, be it the Kaziranga National Park, the Keibul Lamjao National Park in Manipur, the Namdapha National Park in Arunachal Pradesh and many others, spread across this region.

4. Planning for Railway Connectivity Between Northeast India and Myanmar

There is railway connectivity in Northeast India and also in Myanmar. Given the common historical background, it should not be impossible to develop a railway link between India's Northeast and Myanmar, to carry goods to begin with and people later. There are already talks about building a New Delhi-Hanoi railway corridor.

5. Increasing Border Trade Through the Border Trading Points

Already trade is going on between India and Myanmar through trading points such as Moreh in Manipur and Zokhawthar in the Northeastern state of Mizoram. Much of this trade is in the informal sector. Although the official figures for the total trade between India and Myanmar stood at $1.6 billion in 2017-18, this could be much more if the trade was formalised. The Indian government has expressed an interest in developing the Rih-Tiddim-Falam road in Myanmar and thereafter connect it to pre-existing roads in Myanmar. This will go a long way in improving the infrastructure in this part of Myanmar.

6. Reciprocal Relaxation of Entry Norms by the ASEAN Countries

In order to give a fillip to people-to-people ties, the ASEAN countries could consider relaxation of entry norms for Indian tourists visiting the ASEAN countries for tourist purposes. This will go a long way in increasing the flow of people between India and ASEAN.

7. Improving Connectivity within Northeast India will also be Critical

As Northeast India accounts for only around 3.8 per cent of the country's total population, it is very important for the different Northeastern states to pool together on various fronts and there has to be ease of movement between the different Northeastern states. At present, this does not seem to be the case, barring some portions of Assam (especially along the southern banks of the Brahmaputra).

Some proposals have been mooted to increase connectivity in the Northeast-these include a 4000km ringroad to connect the Northeastern states, extending railway connectivity to all the state capitals, putting in place railway connectivity with Myanmar and then restoring the railway connectivity with Bangladesh[2] – which was lost in the wake of the formation of East Pakistan and later on Bangladesh.

One of the highlights of last year's Delhi Dialogue X in New Delhi was the involvement of ministers and officials from the Northeastern states of India. The theme of last year's Delhi Dialogue was 'Strengthening ASEAN-India Maritime Cooperation'. This is significant given the increased focus on the maritime domain by the Modi government.

India has also signed a contract for the development of the Sabang port in Indonesia, which lies at the entrance of the Straits of Malacca and thus is key for India.

8. Improving the Riverine Connectivity

Given the terrain of the region, it is important to improve the riverine connectivity as well. Earlier, the Brahmaputra river used to be an important travel artery for the region, but that is no longer the case. Given the increased importance given to the maritime domain and the use of river routes, this has acquired a renewed focus. As India's relations with Bangladesh improve, such riverine links will become increasingly important.

9. Agreement for Movement of Vehicles

In addition, some kind of an agreement needs to be worked out between India and the ASEAN nations which will allow the movement of vehicles between India and the ASEAN nations like the Bangladesh, Bhutan, India, Nepal (BBIN) agreement (though Bhutan is still not a party to the BBIN agreement).

Connectivity is going to be the key word as far as Northeast India's ties with Japan and ASEAN are concerned. There are already talks going on regarding extending the India-Myanmar-Thailand trilateral highway all the way to Vietnam via Laos and Cambodia.

10. Setting up of Consulates from the ASEAN Nations and Japan in Northeast India

Given the growing connections between NE India and the ASEAN and Japan, it is important that consulates from the ASEAN countries and also from Japan are set up in Northeast India, which will facilitate the coordination process between the ASEAN countries, Japan and Northeast India.

11. Road Connecitivity with ASEAN

Many a times, some states of the Northeast, especially the hill states, get cut-off from the rest of the country/other parts of the Northeast due to natural disasters and/or floods. During times like these, it is important for such states from the Northeast to have road connectivity with the ASEAN countries, especially with countries like Myanmar. In addition, sometimes due to issues like political protests, there are blockades in some parts of the Northeast.

12. High-Speed Rail Connectivity with ASEAN

India is likely to have its own version of the bullet train which will connect Mumbai (India's financial capital) with Ahmedabad in Gujarat. In the future, there could be prospects for the inauguration of a high-speed railway corridor between Northeast India and the national capital, New Delhi and also between Northeast India and the ASEAN countries.

13. Giving Skills to Youngsters from North East India

It is important to give the necessary skills to youngsters from NE India so that they can help find employment in the ASEAN countries and also in Japan. Singapore has already stolen a march over others in this area by signing an MoU with the government of Assam to set up a skills development centre in Guwahati.

Many youths from the Northeastern part of India have found employment in the hospitality sector across India and also in other countries. Keeping in view the opportunities available in countries like Singapore, Malaysia and others, they could look for jobs in these countries as well.

PM Modi while speaking at the India-ASEAN Summit in Nay Pyi Daw in November 2014 noted that "we have embarked on a new economic journey in India. We are emphasizing infrastructure, manufacturing, trade, agriculture, skill development, urban renewal, smart cities. Make in India is a new mission. We are placing as much emphasis on ease of doing business in India as we are on making policies attractive. I invite you to this new environment in India."[3]

14. Completion of the Planned Projects

In addition, one of the most important requirements will be to complete the agreed projects on time because the delivery is as important as the planning. As opposed to Beijing-backed projects, India's record at execution of key projects has been patchy at best. If India is to play its rightful role on the world stage, it must make sure that it is able to deliver key projects on time. For this, it will be important to rope in private players on a big scale. While Indian private sector companies have had a big success in some parts of the world like Africa, they have largely been reticent when it come to the ASEAN.

15. Preparing Country-Specific Plans for the Different ASEAN Countries

New Delhi also needs to adopt a country-specific strategy when it comes to the ASEAN countries instead of a "one-size fits all" approach, while has not yielded the desired results for New Delhi. For example, Cambodia, Myanmar, Laos and Vietnam (CMLV countries) are at a different stage of development as compared to countries like Singapore or Malaysia for that matter.

16. Improving Maritime Connectivity

Improving maritime connectivity will be key as land connectivity is difficult and costly, whereas aerial connectivity will benefit only a select few. In the ancient days, it was by the maritime route that Indian customs and influence spread to various parts of the world and this is the realm that India needs to look at anew.

17. Including Plans for the Development of Adjoining Areas in Myanmar

Any development plans for Northeast India will not work unless steps are taken to undertake development activities in the neighbouring parts of Myanmar too like Chin, Kachin and Sagaing etc. Only then, we will be able to see the full results of the "Act-East Policy". This has to be done in consultation with the government of Myanmar. India under PM Modi has embarked on the "Make in India" initiative. Both ASEAN and Japan can be key partners in the "Make in India" initiative. In terms of demography, both India and ASEAN have young populations. Hence they will be a good match.

18. Joint Collaboration between India-ASEAN-Japan

There could be collaboration between companies from India, ASEAN and Japan in projects across the world, for example in Africa. This could dovetail into initiatives like the India-Japan Asia-Africa Growth Corridor (AAGC). Companies from the ASEAN countries have been at the forefront in sectors like ports and in the light of initiatives like the Sagarmala project-which encourages port-led growth in India-there is immense potential for companies from the ASEAN countries in port development in India, especially given India's long coastline.

19. Promoting Ecologically viable Architecture

Japan has been at the forefront of developing ecofriendly infrastructure solutions, especially given the nature of Japan's geography and the highly-conscious public opinion in the country. Northeast India needs the same kind of infrastructure since this region has suffered from major earthquakes in the past. The region has faced major earthquakes in 1897 and 1950.

20. Joint NE India-Myanmar Special Economic Zones

If there is good connectivity between Northeast India and Myanmar, it could be connected to the Japanese-backed Special Economic Zones in Myanmar. This will help in increasing income levels in Northeast India. Poor infrastructure is one of the main reasons for the economic underdevelopment in this part of the country.

In the future, Northeast India is likely to become the bridge which will link India not only with Southeast Asia, but also to countries like Japan. Here is the only part of India that is physically connected to Southeast Asia and the only part of India, which has had experience of interacting with the Japanese (along with the Andaman and Nicobar Islands). As India gives more teeth to its "Act-East Policy", Northeast India is certainly going to be the bridge between India and ASEAN and also between India and Japan.

Indian External Affairs Minister Sushwa Swaraj noted at the Delhi Dialogue X in July 2018, India and ASEAN (with a combined population of 1.85 billion) account for a quarter of the world's population and have a combined GDP of over US$ 3.8 trillion. While bilateral trade now stands at around US$ 80 billion, "it is expected to reach US$100 billion by 2020."[4]

Northeast India is in the best position to take advantage of the growing cooperation between India, ASEAN and Japan[5]. This is a once-in-a-lifetime opportunity, the likes of which will not come again. It will now depend on the governments and the people of Northeast India, if, and whether, they can rise to the occasion.

NOTES

1. BBC Travel, The Cleanest Village in Asia, available at http://www.bbc.com/travel/story/20160606-the-cleanest-villagein-asia accessed on February 22, 2019.
2. Live Mint, The North East is key for India's ties with Asean available at https://www.livemint.com/Opinion/o4QS DxyenyvZ0QGwX5mwdL/The-North-East-is-key-for-Indias-ties-with-Asean.html accessed on February 22, 2019.
3. Narendra Modi.in, Remarks by the PM at the 12th India-

ASEAN Summit, Nay Pyi Taw, Myanmar, available at https://www.narendramodi.in/remarks-by-the-pm-atthe-12th-india-asean-summit-nay-pyi-tawmyanmar-6878 accessed on February 19, 2019.

4. Ministry of External Affairs, India, Remarks by External Affairs Minister at Delhi Dialogue X, available at https://www.mea.gov.in/Speeches-Statements.htm?dtl/30138/Remarks+by+External+Affairs+Minister+at+Delhi+Dialogue+X+ July+19+2018 accessed on January 17, 2019.

5. The Straits Times, ASEAN and India: 25 years and beyond, available at https://www.straitstimes.com/opinion/aseanand-india-25-years-and-beyond-0 accessed on February 12, 2019.

INDEX

X

Y

PHOTOGRAPHS

A Tori Gate in Japan: There is Similarity of Religious Practices between India and Japan

Similarity of Terrain in North-East India and Japan

Similarity of Topography between Northeast India, ASEAN and Japan

The Mighty Brahmaputra River in Guwahati: This River will be Key for Riverine Connectivity in the Region